SAILED AWAY
AND SURVIVED

CLARE ANN CONWAY

Copyright © 2017 Clare Ann Conway

All rights reserved. No part(s) of this book may be reproduced, distributed or transmitted in any form, or by any means, or stored in a database or retrieval systems without prior expressed written permission of the author of this book.

ISBN: 978-1-5356-0872-5

Acknowledgements

MANY, MANY THANKS TO ALL the people who generously donated their family photos and stories, and made it possible, so I could make this book. I was urged to commemorate all the ordeals and adventures that these families from Ireland went thru. Stories compiled before their existences slipped into the vast repository of those who have died and left no evidence of who they were, what they confronted, or what their victories were. These Irish people had so many hard times that I wanted to remember them in a book for future generation to read and know about. It's very important that history records the stories of how this generation of Irish survived. This is a compilation of stories of original families of Ireland submitted and written by Great Grandchildren, Grandchildren or other family members that wanted their ancestors to be remembered. These are the lives and stories of the people that lived in, Mayo, Cork, Dublin, Clare, Wicklow, Derry, and other counties of Ireland. Many ancestors stayed and died in Ireland but many more chose to go to Australia, England, America, Canada, Argentina, South Africa, or other countries around the World. If we don't keep these memories going, one day the tragedy, desperation and inhumanity will all be forgotten. These are the memories and stories from their descendants.

The Irish Potato Famine

JUST TO SAY SOMETHING ABOUT the Potato Famine. The Potato famine struck Ireland late August 1845. The potatoes suddenly turned black. The cause was an air born fungus - Phytophthora. Ireland saw the potato crop fail (1800-1845) in the past, but it was regionally. But in this famine, crops died nationally. Also by 1846 supplies of corn meal were exhausted. The potato crop had never failed for 2 consecutive years. But this blight was there to stay and 3 out of the following 4 years would be a potato disaster. During 1845-1850 800,000 Irish people died of starvation or famine related diseases, such as Typhus, Scurvy and Dysentery. The population of 8 1/2 Million, over 1 Million died, approximately 2 Million emigrated to other countries for a better life. Many, many died on coffin ships. This was a very horrible time in Irish History. There were of course, many other reasons that people died during this time. People were evicted from their homes by the British, homes that they built themselves of stone, but were left to starve in the streets by cruel landlords, just to mention some of the hardships of the Irish people of this time- frame.

The Workhouses, there were 163 workhouses in total. If people could not support themselves, they could come into the workhouse. Here they would do some work in return for food. One of the cruelest aspects of the workhouse was that family members were split up into separate quarters. Children aged two or less could stay with their mothers. Sometimes, family members never saw each other again. It was starvation or the workhouse. There were a large, number of children in the workhouses. In 1850 up to 120,000 children. Many children who survived the famine grew up in workhouse. Hungry and dirty. They are not to be forgotten!

Contents

Acknowledgements iii
The Irish Potato Famine v
James Reid 1
Margaret Theresa Doherty 3
Edward H Wiggins 5
William Drummy 8
Hannah Amilia O'Maley 10
Thomas Tunney 15
Philip Quinn 18
James B Rafferty 20
Thomas Long 23
Katherine (Kate) Marie Hayes 26
Mary Stanton 29
Richard Donoghue 31
Margaret Molloy 34
John McCarthy 36
James Hughes 38
John Joseph Cunningham 40
Denis Hamill 42
Florence Harrington 44
Elizabeth (Ellen) Harkins 46
Honora Convey 49
Michael Sullivan 51
Martin Joseph Durkin 53

Margaret Swanton	54
James Joseph Kearney	57
Thomas Barry Moriarty M. D. R.A.M	59
Ellen McGovern	60
Hugh Beggan	62
Mary Kelly	64
Helen Browne	67
Thomas Francis Flaherty	70
Patrick McHugh	72
John S Sullivan	74
Mary Molly	77
Ann Jane Marks	80
Yehuda Maisha Shillman	83
John Hoban	86
Oliver Nash Moriarty Lt. Col.	87
William Watson	88
Delia Bridget Coleman	91
Joseph Redmond	93
Bernard Feeney	94
Dorinda Florence (Dot) Moriarty	95
John Darcy	96
Annie Molly	98
Catharine Feeney	102
James Mullin	103

James Kelaher	104
Patrick Joseph Conway	107
Thomas O'Brien	109
Catherine McVeigh	110
Mary Ann Linden	113
Patrick Green	115
Annie Lennon	117
Cornelius Lyhane	118
Margaret ("Maggie") Cunniffe	120
Martin Fadden	123
Anne Brennan	125
Thomas Clancy	126
Dennis Conway	128
James Joseph Costello	131
Maurice Histon	133
Mary McQueeny	134
Michael Hamilton Lennon	136
Michael (Gow) Sullivan	137
Our Lady of Knock Queen of Ireland	138
Novena To Our Lady Of Knock	141
Mary Agnes O'Leary	142
Annie Whelan	143
Ann Murphy	144
Mary Hopkins	146
Peter Ambrose Lennon	147
Daniel Gallagher	148
Lawrence (Larry) Newell	151
Martin Michael Morrison	153
Michael Conway	154
Catherine (Kate) Connell	156

Anna Frances Maguire	158
Martin Logan	160
Maurice Hugh O'Connor	161
Robert Burrows	162
Ellen O'Sullivan	164
Patrick Bannon	166
Isaac Langford	168
Patrick Gallagher	170
Ann (Nancy) Mulryan	173
Catherine Burns	175
Michael J Callaghan	176
James Patrick Lawlor	179
Joseph McClare	182
Dominick McGrail	185
Bridget Snee	188
Jeremiah Darby Mee	190
Patrick Grady	192
Katherine Celia Smyth	194
John Pickett	196
George Evans Lowe	201
Ellen Marie (Nellie) Leahy	205
Catherine (Kitty) Cochrane	209
Martin Neary	212
Katherine Flanagan	214
James Carlile McCoan	216
James McDonald	218
John Church	223
Gavin Shaw	226
Sarah Willis	228
James Paul Geraghty	230

John Joseph Sheehan	232
Michael Pollard	234
Elizabeth "Lizzy" Lennon	236
Jeremiah Sullivan	242
Michael Connell	244
Francis Stirling McCracken	247
Patrick Joseph Sheehan	250
Harris Daniel Zvi Noyek	253
John H Gaffney	259
Peter Kavanagh	264
Margaret Anderson	266
Mamie Allen	268
Hugh Hodges	271
Kate Sheridan	275
Thomas Joseph Donovan Sr	279
Bridget (Bessie) O'Hara	282
James Patrick Dinnen	283
John Moran	286
Thomas McCracken	288
Joseph McCracken	290
Charlotte Glass	292
John Murphy	296
Ellen Maher	298
Mary Agnes Joyce	301
Thomas Moore	302
Bridget McQueeny	304
Margaret (Maggie) Cahill	306
Dorinda Florence (Dot) Moriarty	307
Elizabeth (Eliza) McQueeny	308
Thomas Adams	310

Alexander Dunn 312
- Just wondering -... 316
Thousands are sailing by Andy Irvine 318

James Reid

born 12/25/1883
Knappabeg, Westport, County Mayo Ireland
Parents: James Reid, Catherine Malley

THE REID FAMILY LIVED IN the town of Knappabeg, Westport, County Mayo. It is on the south-east corner of Clew Bay, an inlet of the Atlantic Ocean on the west coast of Ireland.

James Reid left Ireland and traveled to America and arrived at Ellis Island, New York, New York sometime around 1912-1915. He then moved on to Chicago, Illinois, looking for work, on the south side, were a lot of Irish lived. James would take in single Irishmen and Irish families who just arrived to Chicago. Giving them a place to stay while they got established.

He met Anna McKeon and on June 2, 1919, they married and had four children. His daughter Veronica Reid Cagle is still alive today March 7, 2016 at 87 years old. James died on March 3, 1962 at the home of his daughter Veronica Cagle, 8841 S Natoma Ave, Oak Lawn, Illinois.

DONATED BY HIS GRANDSON PAUL CAGLE 2/3/1916
BORN IN CHICAGO ILLINOIS, LIVES IN NAPLES FLORIDA,
RETIRED POLICEMAN FROM COOK COUNTY, ILLN.
MARRIED WITH 2 CHILDREN

Margaret Theresa Doherty

born 1848
Ballytweedy, County Antrim, Northern Ireland
Parents: Daniel Doherty, Margaret White

MARGARET THERESA DOHERTY WAS BORN in 1848 in a small farmhouse in the townland of Ballytweedy, County Antrim, in the middle of the famine years. She was the youngest daughter, of a Roman Catholic Father and Presbyterian Mother. Her Mothers family live in the nearby town of Ballyrobin. (Margaret's father, William White, was a cousin of Field Marshall Sir George White of Ladysmith Fame).

Margaret Doherty was initially educated at the local Ballyrobin Primary School but showed so much promise in her English class that she was selected to attend the Convent of Mercy School in Belfast, to prepare her for teacher training. In 1864 at the age of 16 years old, she was appointed as Junior Assistant Teacher at a small country school in Aghagallon, County Antrim, Northern Ireland. She remained working there till she married.

In 1869 Margaret met and married Hugh Pender, who was a calico printer. Margaret and Hugh then moved to live beside the large Printing Works where he lived and worked in Whitewell Village near Belfast. They had eight children, three boys and five girls. Seven of whom lived into adulthood. Margaret began submitted poems and short stories to local and national newspapers with some success. Her poems regularly won prizes in the newspapers and periodicals that she entered. The prize money was a useful supplement to the family's finances. In 1880, she was asked, by the Editor of a Dublin newspaper to write a story to serialize in the weekly paper, which she did. This story which was published over the following ten weeks, proved so popular that she continued writing stories. She wrote about Irish historical events and personalities for publication, over the next forty years.

Margaret became one of the most respected Irish Authors of her day with many of her writings, later being published in book form. She was much sought after as a public speaker on local political platforms. Margaret was a strong supporter of Irish Home rule and spoke at many political rallies. In her day, Margaret was considered something of a firebrand of her day, with anti-British speeches sometimes being quoted by MP's in the British House of Commons.

Right up to her death, Margaret T. Pender published hundreds of short stories, serials and poems in National newspaper which were copied to American and Australian periodicals and sold very well. Margaret Doherty Pender died on St. Patrick's Day in 1920 at the age of 72 years old. She was buried in the outskirts of her beloved Belfast.

DONATED 3/14/2016 BY GREAT GRANDNEPHEW ALEX MILLAR
BORN AND LIVES IN BELFAST, NORTHERN IRELAND.
　WIDOWED, RETIRED, 2 CHILDREN

Edward H Wiggins

born 6/19/1855
Newtown Butler, County Fermanagh, Northern Ireland
Parents: John William Wiggins 1820-1880;
Mary Unknown 1822-1920

EDWARD WIGGINS WAS ONE OF eleven children that grew up on a working farm. The farm house in Newtown Butler consisted of a three room, stone house with a loft and it had a chimney on each end of the house. There was a step ladder, used to go up to the loft and the girls slept in the loft. The loft was one large room with a small glass windows on either end of the house. The glass windows were very little because the farm owner was taxed on the amount of glass they had in the farmhouse. The house, consisted of three rooms with clay floors that was packed down hard. The floors were generally swept cleans, with what was called a heather broom. The three rooms were, a large living room, kitchen and the sitting room. The large room was occupied by the parents and the sitting room had 2 beds in it were the boys slept.

In the morning, Edward and his sibling eat oatmeal porridge and buttermilk, washed up in cold water outside on a bench. Then they tended to farm chores. Dinner consisted of bacon, turnip, and cabbage. On days when there was no cabbage, they eat a large basket of boiled potatoes with the jackets on. Fresh meat was unheard of.

There was an old well on the farm called the Spew Well; this was supposed to be one of the reasons why the people in that vicinity lived so long. The water was rather peculiar. It had a Sulphur taste, but after you got used to it, the flavor as rather pleasant.

At the age of 19 years old, Edward Wiggins decided to leave Ireland and go to another country where there were more job opportunities. His parents wanted him to go to either Canada or America. In the Spring of 1873 Edward left Ireland for Canada with two friends. It was a twelve, day voyage by boat and the trip went very well until their ship reached the Gulf of the St. Lawrence River. Here they were delayed by frozen ice for four days.

When their passage was freed up, the ship continued onto Quebec, Canada. Landing in Quebec, Edward and his friends took a railroad trip and arrived in Ottawa, Canada. In Ottawa Edward got a job in a lumber camp for the winter and the job was more than he could tolerate. So finally, in the middle of the night Edward packed up all his belongings and left. He then secured a position as a night clerk at the Daniel Hotel, where he stayed until the winter of 1875.

Edward had an Uncle John McKeever, on his father's side, that lived, in Michigan in America and Edward decided to go visit the Uncle and stayed with the Uncle until June. He then traveled to Chicago Illinois, but didn't stay there long and continued, on to Philadelphia Pennsylvania.

Almost everyone was going to Philadelphia for the Centennial of 1876. In Philadelphia Edward secured a position at the Atlas Hotel, procuring guests from the railroad station for the hotel. Edward worked at the Atlas Hotel until the closing of the Centennial, then he took a job in Milbourne Mills, as a shipper, which was at 63rd and Market Streets. This was a very small plant, with just a few employees. He was paid $7.50 a week and he work at this Mill for 24 years.

In June 1881 Edward joined the Arcturus Lodge of Odd Fellows, where he met men of the finest character. He became an active member and worked in every capacity he could to help- out and stayed a member for 30 years.

Edward did go back to Ireland in 1889 to see his mother. He found her sitting in the same old rocking chair that she had been sitting in for generation.

In Philadelphia Edward met Isabella Montgomery and they married and had seven children, William, Florence, Edward, Albert, Isabel, Herbert, and Harwood. Eventually Edward was making $9.00 a week and when he was able, to save $1,000, he purchased a lot of land on Race Street and built his own home.

In 1892, Edward's wife Isabella became very ill and he took her to every doctor and hospital for help and treatment. She was diagnosed with Cancer of the liver by Dr. Lelaine, at University Hospital. Dr. Lelaine told Edward to take his wife home for her days were short.

Isabella died on Dec 5, 1892 and Edward was left to raise five boys and two girls, the oldest was 13 years old, by himself. Nine months later his son Herbert passed away.

In 1901 Edward left Milbourne Mills and went to work for the Post Office, where he stayed working at until April 1928. In 1919 when he was 65 years old, he met Sarah E MacCullough. On Thanksgiving Eve 1919 they married.

Edward Wiggins died at his home residence in Philadelphia, PA. in 1933 at 78 years old.

This story was from Edward Wiggins own personal Autobiography passed down to family members.

DONATED 6/28/2016 BY GR GREAT GRANDDAUGHTER
  MONTE ELIZABETH WIGGINS STACK
BORN IN MIAMI FLORIDA, LIVE IN GEORGIA
RETIRED, MARRIED

William Drummy

born 1841
Cork, County Cork, Ireland
Parents: Nicholas Drummy born 1820, Parish of Belmont,
Bellincollig, County Cork;
Julie Buttimer born 1820, County Cork Ireland

On Sept 23, 1853 William Drummy departed Ireland for Liverpool England. From England, he immigrated to America and he arrived in Boston, Massachusetts.

On Nov 27, 1860 William enlisted in the U.S. Army. He was listed as being 5ft. 6ins tall and a Roman Catholic. He was enlisted as a Private, Laborer, to Company A of the 2nd U.S. Light Artillery where he served for 5yrs.

This is important because this Company A was the first that fired the shots at the Battle of Gettysburg on July 1, 1863. After the War, William traveled to Northern Kentucky, to Cynthiana Kentucky, which is where he had relatives that had lived and farmed in Cynthiana for 10 years. In Kentucky William became a farmer.

In 1866 he met Ellen Louise Ahern. Ellen Ahern was born Dec 19, 1846 in County Waterford, Ireland. She immigrated to America in 1866 and arrived at Ellis Island, New York. From here she traveled to Kentucky to meet William. They married on July 5, 1868 in St. Mary's, Covington County, Kentucky. William and Ellen had eight children.

In about 1890 the family moved to Cincinnati, Hamilton Ohio. William Drummy died on May 25, 1898 and his wife Ellen Ahern

Drummy died on Dec 15, 1918 in a Retirement Home of Diabetes and they were buried at St. Joseph's New Cemetery, Cincinnati Ohio.

DONATED 3/19/2016 BY GREAT GRANDSON
 TIMOTHY PATRICK HENNESSEY
BORN IN CINCINNATI OHIO, MARRIED, LIVES IN NORTHWEST FLORIDA

Hannah Amilia O'Maley

born 1812
County Mayo, Ireland

IRELAND WAS STRUGGLING WITH WIDESPREAD food shortages which caused illness and despair across the nation. In later years, this led to the great famine. Hannah O' Maley immigrated to England to pursue a better life. Hanna was a very attractive woman of 4'11" tall with dark brown hair and hazel eyes.

In England, Hannah met Samuel Cummins, who was born in 1806. They married at St. Mary's Church, Lamberth, Middlesex England on Dec 16, 1827 and they had seven children from 1828-1843. In 1841 the family lived in Middlesex England in the parish of St. George in Hanover Square. Samuel and his eldest son, Samuel, were laborers. Sometime around 1846 Samuel deserted his family for another woman and left for America. After that Hannah changed her name back to O'Maley.

This was not an easy life for Hannah, on Aug 17, 1847, at the age of 34 years, she is tried at Central Criminal Court for larceny, for stealing a woman's gown valued at 2 shillings and she had a previous conviction of felony of receiving a stolen watch. She was found guilty and sentenced to seven years and was transported to Van Diemen's Land, Australia.

On July 21,1847 Hannah arrived at Van Diemens Land, Hobart Town, Tasmania, Australia on the ship S.S. Asia with five of her seven children, Emily, Hannah, Amelia, John, Joseph. The two eldest children were left in England with Hannah's sister Margaret. All, of the children were vaccinated during the voyage. Upon their arrival the children were sent to the Queen's Orphan School at St. John's Park, New Town. Her eldest daughter, Emily, was discharged into the care of George Salier of Hobart on Aug 11, 1847 as a servant in his home.

Hannah underwent seven months training in domestic duties on the Anson, a probation station for female convicts moored on the River Derwent. She was instructed in the ways of doing laundry, cleaning and repairing clothing and linen. Later she was assigned to work for private individuals: Mr. Boyes of New Town in 1848, Mr. Beal in 1848, and Mr. Bonney in 1849.

However, Hannah was struggling to adjust to her new life in Tasmania, she was found absent without leave on two occasions, Aug 1848, and Nov 1848. She was sentenced to four months, hard labor in both incidences. Then in Oct 1849 she was found intoxicated and she had assaulted a constable, in the course, of conducting his duties, and received seven months of labor. Hannah served the three sentences at the Cascades Female Factory, totaling fifteen months.

In an attempt, to get her life back on track, Hannah applied for a ticket of leave, but it was denied on Aug 20,1850. Hannah met a new man, Thomas Livesley, a free- man. Hannah applied to married but it was refused.

On Dec 24 1850 she successfully obtained a Ticket of Leave and the 1st of her children, Hannah age 13years, was released into her care from the Orphanage on Jan 27,1851. Hannah's second child Amelia was discharged from Queen's Orphanage on Dec 1852, she was 16 years of age and she was release to Reverend Ewing Chaplain of St. John's, as his servant.

Things were looking brighter for Hannah, as she remarried to Thomas Livesley on Feb 28,1853 in Hobart at the Independent Chapel at Brisbane St. She was also given a certificate of Freedom on Sept 3,1853 and her youngest child John, age 9 was released from the Orphanage. Her last son Joseph to be released on Jan 1855.

From 1860-1877 Hannah was charged with various offenses. The marriage of Hannah and Thomas broke down and they were living separately by 1866. By 1879 the Orphanage had closed and became the New Town Pauper establishment, which was for the poor and ill, suffering from a range of disabilities. On June 1874 Hannah was admitted to the New Town Pauper Establishment. She was an alcoholic and in declining health. She stayed at New Town till 1883 and was released to one of her daughters, Emily, or Amelia.

Hannah Amelia O'Maley died on July 24,1884 of Senility (weak with age) at the age of 72 years old and buried on July 26,1884 in the pauper section at Cornelia Bay Cemetery, Hobart Town, Tasmania, Australia.

DONATED 7/10/2016 BY GR GRANDDAUGHTER KATE BOUSFIELD
LIVES IN PERTH, WESTERN AUSTRALIA
MARRIED, 5 CHILDREN

Thomas Tunney

born 1866
DerryKillew Parish of Cushough, County Mayo Ireland

THOMAS TUNNEY WAS A TAILOR and Farmer, 5' 7"tall with black hair. He was a Catholic and spoke fluent Gaelic.

He married Margaret Mullroe, who was born in 1880 from the nearby town of Greenhaun, Tourmakeady, Westport, County Mayo. Margaret Mullroe was 5' 5" tall, a Catholic, spoke fluent Gaelic and was a very loyal to her family and country. This was the time of Matchmaking and their deal was done in 1900 at The Pattern in Leenane, County Mayo. Leenane Village is situated at the head of the Killary Harbor, nestled under the Maamtrasna and Maamturk Mountains, just 1/2 hour from Westport. This was the first time they had laid eyes on each other.

Thomas was twenty-one years older than his bride. Thomas and Margaret married and had 5 children; Patrick b-1887, Michael b-1888, Mary b-1892, Thomas b-1894, and Peter b-1897.

Margaret played the Melodeon, a type of small button accordion. She taught her son Michael to play it also. Michael played the fiddle, melodeon and the accordion. He joined the IRB Pipeband in Carrowkenny, Westport, County Mayo.

On 1916 the band had the honor of heading the parade on St. Patrick's Day. They marched from the Octagon to Westport Railway Station to meet the O'Rahilly who was coming to address a meeting in Westport that day. (The O'Rahilly was killed in Dublin during Easter Rising only a matter of weeks later). In 1918, Michael Tunney led the band at the trial of Mr. Ned Moane from Westport and William O'Malley from Newport, on that day the band was attacked by the Royal Irish Constabulary (R.I.C) on Castlebar street. Some band members were so severely beaten that they had to be hospitalized. Their drums and fifes which they used in self-defense, that event saw the permanent debanding of the band.

Margaret's son Patrick was a Poet and a Songwriter. He was heavily involved in the Irish Republican Brotherhood, with his brother Michael. Patrick married Nora Dunne of CarrowKennedy, Westport in 1917 and they raised 10 children. He then joined the Irish Volunteer movement at its inception, this began a life where he would see the iron bars and barbed wire of, no fewer, then, twelve different jails in England, Wales, and Ireland. Patrick spent many years on the run and imprisoned for disobeying the British authorities the "occupied' army of the time.

On the March 22,1921, early in the morning, the Black & Tans arrived at the Tunney home and to their surprise they found Patrick Tunney there. They had believed him to be under lock and key in Galway jail. However, Tunney had been granted a ten, day parole from Galway jail because his wife just gave birth to daughter, Margaret Mary Tunney.

The Black & Tans pinned Patrick at gun point against the gable wall of his home with the intent to execute him on the spot. And thanks to the cries of a tiny newborn baby from within and the pleading of the family, Patrick was spared. Patrick Tunney was advised to return to the 'safety' of Galway jail.

The Black & Tans went up to the bedroom and pulled the bed clothes off his wife's bed, in case she was hiding a fugitive. The grandmother, Margaret Mullroe Tunney, boldly refused to converse with the Black & Tans other than Gaelic, which they didn't understand. They hit her with the butt of their rifles and knocked her against the dresser, injuring her. They smashed her spinning wheel and burned it in the fire.

Their son Michael died in Dublin at the age of 89 years, buried with his wife Kate. Son Thomas was a farmer who died in 1970 and was buried in Cushlough Parish Cemetery. Their son Peter J. Tunney (also known as Peadar in Westport markets and Joe in USA) emigrated to America about 1922 to New York City, New York. He was buried in a pauper's grave. Patrick died in 1951 and was buried in the Cushlough Cemetery. His funeral, was met by thousands of people from Westport and Drummin. His old comrades of the I.R.A. rendered full military honors at the graveside where, an oration was, delivered by Brigadier. Ed. Moane, West Mayo Brigade.

Thomas Tunney died in 1915 and his wife Margaret Mullroe Tunney died in 1949 at the age of 85 years and they were buried together in Chushlough Parish Cemetery.

DONATED 11/5/2016 BY GREAT GRANDSON BRENDAN TUNNEY
BORN IN ROCHESTER, NEW YORK, LIVES IN ROCHESTER, NEW YORK
IT TECHNICIAN, MARRIED, 1 DAUGHTER AISLING TUNNEY

Philip Quinn

born 7/14/1801
Goland, Stranolar, County Donegal Ireland

PHILIP QUINN EMIGRATED FROM IRELAND to America in 1822, landing in Eastport Maine on Aug 1,1822. He continued, on and settled in Portland Maine were there was a very large Irish population for him to find work.

In Portland Philip met Mary Ann Weeks, who was a native of Portland. Mary Ann Weeks was born Feb 28, 1807, the daughter of Philip Weeks and Martha (Patty) Hodgkins. They married in Aug 1823 and had nine children.

In June 1834 Philip became a Naturalized U.S. Citizen. In 1837 his home was at Fore Jones Row. He was an active member of St. Dominic's Church and vice-president of the Hibernian Benevolent Society in 1839. Philip was a trader and grocer and owned his own store and boarding house, the "O'Connell House".

As a leader of the Portland Irish community, and friend of the Boston Pilot's editor, Philip acted as an agent receiving letters from Irish families seeking lost family members.

Philip was taken to court many times for selling illegal liquor. In 1846 Neal Dow, who was responsible for passing the Maine Alcohol Prohibition Law, encountered Philip in his frantic war on Rum sellers, especially Irish Rum sellers. Philip Quinn, called "One of the most corrigible Rum sellers in the City", declared that Neal Dow was trying to make a beggar of him from all the fines he had to pay out dues to the infractions of the Liquor Law. After several years of court battles, Philip disappeared on July 4,1853 and was discovered drowned in Portland Harbor near Fort Preble. Philip Quinn was buried in South Portland Maine at Calvary Cemetery. His wife Mary Ann Weeks Quinn was buried there on July 23,1860.

Donated 6/7/2016 by Great Granddaughter, Valerie H. Burrows Born in Oakland California, Lives in Sacramento Calif works as a Facility Administrator and Theatre

James B Rafferty

born 4/12/1825
Dungannon, County Tyrone, Northern Ireland

JAMES RAFFERTY, A ROMAN CATHOLIC, and his brother Hugh left Ireland because of the famine in Ireland. They also have a sister Bernadette who stayed in Ireland.

In 1845 James and Hugh went to England where James learned a boot making trade. From England, they went up to Scotland and learned some of the Railroad Trade. They then booked passage to America and arrived in Boston, Massachusetts. James and Hugh worked in Boston until 1860, when the American Civil War broke out.

In this time, seven Southern States declared session for the U.S (union), and united to form the Confederate States of America. Text books say it was a conflict over slavery that caused the Civil War.

James and Hugh left Boston Mass. and moved up to Portage, Prince Edward Island, Canada. In 1862 Hugh goes back to Boston Mass, it was too cold in Canada for him, and he then joined the Civil War.

James met Mary Ann Bulger, who was also from Ireland. They married and had three girls, Mary, Ann, and Ellen Margaret. (Later in life, the girls all marry and move to America). James bought a large farm in Portage, lot 11, PEI, Canada to become a farmer.

From the trade jobs, he learned in Scotland, James also becomes a Foreman over a crew that built the Prince Edward Island Railroad. He was a very intelligent man, almost a scholar. He was a great reader and speaker. Anyone looking for information on land law went to James for help. He was also an excellent Step dancer. James Rafferty died in 1914 at his farm where he was also buried, in Potage, Prince Edward Island, Canada.

Donated 4/28/2016 by Gr Granddaughter Ellen Rafferty Lives in Summerside, Prince Edward Island, Canada Married, 2 children, Retired Postmaster at Canada Post Corporation

Thomas Long

born March 1843
Clough Jordan, County Tipperary, Ireland
Parents: Thomas Long, Mary Burke

THIS IS THE STORY OF Thomas Long, who confessed to killing John Ellis on his deathbed. Thomas Long told his daughter before he died that he was the man who killed John Ellis, the murder that the Cormack Brothers were hung for.

In March 1858, two brothers, Daniel 19 years old and William 23 years old were executed for the murder of John Ellis. They both pleaded for clemency and Daniel, stated he had no part or hand in the death. John Ellis was a known womanizer and known to have had a relationship with both Kitty and Nancy Cormack. The police assumed that the Cormack's had killed Ellis to stop Kitty Cormack from ending up pregnant.

Thomas Long was a Tall 6'7", laborer in Tipperary, Ireland. He was just in his late teens when he did the murder and left Ireland three months later, never to return. Thomas left Ireland aboard the ship S.S. Colorado and arrived at Castle Gardens, New York in April 1859. From here Thomas continued, on and settled in Troy, New York.

He enlisted in to the Civil War and was listed on the Troy, New York, Civil War Muster Roll on Oct 1864. He was listed as absent because he was sick at the Port Hospital in Fort McHenry, Maryland.

In 1871 he met Ellen Burke. Ellen was also from County Tipperary, Ireland. They married and had five children, Catharine, Nora, Margaret,

William, and Mary. Thomas was an attendant at St. Joseph Catholic Church and a member of the married men's Sodality.

In 1875 Thomas was a Police Officer for the City of Troy, New York for a short, period, of time. In 1900 Thomas and his family lived at 2 Trenton St. Troy, New York and he was a day laborer. He retired because of his failing health.

Thomas Long died on Oct 9, 1910, Thursday, in Troy, New York at his residence at 152 Jackson St. At the time of his death, Thomas was a caretaker at Prospect Park for a short time.

DONATED 6/25/2016 BY GREAT GRANDSON, MATTHEW COSTELLO
BORN IN ROCHESTER, NEW YORK, SINGLE, DISABLED
WAS A RESTAURANT MANAGER, ALSO WORKED FOR KODAK, MAKING FILM.

Katherine (Kate) Marie Hayes

born 3/18/1876
County Limerick, Ireland

IN 1898 KATHERINE (KATE) HAYES emigrated from Ireland to America and landed in Castle Garden, New York. Castle Garden, New York was the port of arrival for all ships bringing immigrants from other countries. Years later New York built Ellis Island for the immigrants to depart off their Ship and register in. Kate continued, on and goes to live with her parent's relatives, who lived in Marshallberg, North Carolina.

It was here in North Carolina Kate meets John Eason Willis a native of Marshallberg. John is a very tall handsome man. John Willis was born April 6, 1868 to George L Willis and Mary Davis Willis. Both his parents were born in the same town of Marshallberg. John loved to fish, he was a Fisherman and a Whaler. He fished for the Whales, to sell for the oil and he fished and caught many different variety of fish for the Market.

Kate and John were married in the first Catholic Church ever built in Craven North Carolina with a Catholic Priest on Dec 26, 1903. And for a while, they lived in Craven, in what were called Row Houses or Railroad houses. Houses build side by side with on common wall with windows in the front and a front door and the same in the back. A back door and windows looking out the backyard. There could be 20 houses built side by side or 50 houses built side by side.

Kate was very unhappy living in Craven, she did not like the culture or environment they lived in. She told John and in 1910 they moved and lived in Carteret, Smyrma, North Carolina and they had 3 daughters, Mary, Anna and Rita. They found they needed a bigger home and decided to move to Troy New York. John's younger sister Ida moves with them. They live at 188 10th St. Troy, Rensselaer, New York. Kate raised the girls and was a housekeeper. Their older daughter Mary went to school and became a nurse. Kate always had a beautiful large flower garden and a large bountiful vegetable garden. She was happiest when gardening. Kate was the neighborhood fashion plate, wearing the finest dresses, always with her hat, gloves, and pocketbook.

By 1940, Kate and John had now moved to 184 10th St. Troy, New York, and had moved in with their youngest daughter Rita, who had married and had a son William. Rita's husband was William DeCelle and Kate and John liked him very much.

Kate's husband John Eason Willis died of a stroke in 1947. Kate Hayes Willis died of Pneumonia in 1958 at the age of 95years. They were both buried in St. Mary's Cemetery, Troy, Rensselaer Co. New York.

DONATED 6/5/2016 BY GRANDDAUGHTER MARY DECELLE STEWART
BORN IN TROY NEW YORK, LIVES IN SPRING HILL FLORIDA,
  RETIRED PARALEGAL
2 DAUGHTERS, 1 SON, 5 GRANDCHILDREN, 1 GREAT GRANDDAUGHTER

Mary Stanton

born 1/6/1880
Clookeen, Kilmeena, Westport, County Mayo, Ireland
Parents: Thomas Johannas Stanton born 1845
Carrowholly, Westport, County Mayo, Ireland. He was a
Farmer owning his own land. Died 1930
Catherine Scahill born-1850 Clooken, Kilmeena, Mayo
Ireland She died 1895 Carrowholly, Westport, County
Mayo. They had seven children

MARY STANTON LIVED IN CARROWHOLLY and would have attended Carrowholly, National School. She immigrated to America on the ship, S.S. Catalonia to Ellis Island, New York in 1895. Mary played her squeeze box on the ship to entertain people. She has a plague on the wall at Ellis Island with her name on it. Mary, was sponsored by her cousin James Fadden to come to America, to Brookline Massachusetts. Arriving in Boston, Mass. Mary continued, on to the home of her cousin James Fadden, at Pearl St. Brookline, Mass.

Looking for work, Mary knocked on doors for days and days, to ask if she could do the laundry or cook the meals. Mary was an excellent cook. She finally got a job as a cook for the Head of the Atlantic and Pacific Tea Co. This was a very large chain grocery store across America. Every Christmas the Head of the A&P would send Mary the largest turkey he could find with all the fixing to go with it. Fruits and vegetables, pies and cranberry juice and cider for a family of eleven.

She married Michael Conway, who she knew from back in Loughloon, Westport, County Mayo, Ireland. Michael also lived on Pearl St. in Brookline, Mass. Michael Conway came to America aboard the Ship S.S. Etruria in 1893 in New York City, New York. Michael worked for the Town of Brookline, Parks Department, Digging ditches and roads for the city. They married on Sept 26, 1900 in St. Mary's Catholic Church, Brookline, Mass. They lived at 18 Aspinwall Ave. Brookline, Mass, it was a duplex and the mortgage was in Mary's name. Mary had eleven children, seven that lived to adult. In her kitchen, she had two cast iron stoves, for her cooking and baking.

Mary spoke with a thick brogue and she wore her hair up in a bun. She took in roomers to help supplement her income. One tenant was a Bootlegger during Prohibition time. She also had tenants on the others side of the duplex until her son Leo got married. Then Leo and his wife Marguarite Sprague lived on the other side. All the bills were in Mary's name. She bought the first family car for her son Thomas and paid $300 for it. She had a cemetery plot that buried fifteen people. Half of the plot belonged to her son-in-law, Stephen Quinn, who was married to Mary's oldest daughter Mary Conway Quinn.

Mary Stanton Conway died in a Nursing Home on 3/30/1963 in Brookline Mass. of a Cerebral Hemorrhage and Congestive Heart Failure. She was buried with her husband Michael Conway at St. Joseph's Cemetery in Jamaica Plain, Mass.

DONATED ON 2/23/2016 BY GRANDDAUGHTER CLARE CONWAY BORN IN NORTH QUINCY, MASS. SINGLE,
RETIRED TO SPRING HILL, FLORIDA

Richard Donoghue

born 3/2/1812
Waterford, County Cork, Ireland
Baptisted 4/6/1814 St. Mary's Parish, County Tipperary,
Ireland
Parents: Thomas O'Donoghue, Bridgid Flynn

IN AUG 1835, RICHARD DONOGHUE arrived at Cape Town, South Africa from County Cork, Ireland. Sometime after he arrived he joined the Military. About this time, his name was changed, and the O was dropped, probably to sound more British.

He arrived with the 25th Inniskelling Regiment then disembarked in Algoa Bay. (Algoa Bay is a wide inlet along the South African East Coast. 425 miles (683 kilometers) east of the Cape of Good Hope). They then continued, on to Grahamstown which is the largest town and a military outpost founded to secure the British influenced in the Cape Colony against the Xhosa people. The regiment arrived at a time when the Peace Treaty concluding the Sixth Frontier War was in the process of ratification. Richard's regiment relieved troops on the frontier, and were to deal with the isolated raids which continued for some time after the formal declaration of peace. At first Richard was stationed at Fort Wilshire on the West Band of the Kieskama River. He remained in the Army until he was discharged at Grahamstown in 1844.

A number, of useful citizens were added to the South African population in the form of discharged soldiers. Many either earned their discharge or bought them. Richard's wife, Ellen arrived shortly after Richard with their son Henry b-1834, born in Nenagh, County Tipperary, Ireland. All, of their other children were born in South Africa, Margaret b-1838, Jane b-1840, and Elizabeth b-1844.

His wife Ellen died at Fort Peddie on Oct 1844. Richard then met and married a widow, Ann Hawkins, she bore him three children; Anne b-1846, Charles Richard b-1848, and Julia b-1849. Ann had two other children: Mary Jane Hawkins b-1894, and Edwin Hawkins who was born 1841.

In 1847 Richard took his family to the Natal, a British colony in south-eastern South Africa. With his wife, Ann, they boarded the ship S.S. Mazeppa, on which the Port Captains list shows the Donoghues and six children. At first the family settled in Pietermaritzburg, which is the capital and second largest city of Natal, South Africa. Here, Richard, was able, to purchase property at 57 Burger Street, Pietermaritzburg. In 1848 Richard applied for a land grant, under a recent proclamation offering land to discharge sailors and he was granted 12 acres. The Grant specified that he had to occupy or cultivate within 6 months. Richard went and selected his land and proceeded to occupy it, but found the land so full with stones that he could not use a plough.

In 1849, he moved to Durban, which was the largest town in the Colony of Natal, and he purchased the property of the Sun Inn and became a lodging housekeeper. It was very difficult making a living and supporting his family in this harsh environment of those days and in 1851 Richard went insolvent.

With his family, he returned to Pietermaritzburg and he started working as a "Car Man" or Carter and venturing throughout the country on various transport-riding journeys. At, this time, he also took an appointment as a Quartermaster-Sergeant in the short-lived expedition sent by the Natal Lieutenant Governor to the Orange River sovereignty to assist the government of the Cape with the Eighth Frontier War. This expedition, got no further than the Umtamvuna River, when it was ordered back to Natal by the Cape Governor, Sir Harry Smith. In 1851, he secured a position as a wagon conductor for the expedition being sent, by the Natal Government, to Major Warren in the Orange River sovereignty, who was expecting trouble with the Basuto.

(The Gun War, also known as the Basuto War, was an 1880-1881 conflict in the British territory of Basutoland (present-day Lesotho) in Southern Africa, fought between Cape Colony forces and rebellious Basotho chiefs over the right of natives to bear arms). A peace treaty was signed with Basotho chiefs in 1881, in which colonial authorities conceded most of the points in dispute. The land remained in Basotho hands and the nation enjoyed unrestricted access to firearms in exchange for a national one-time indemnity of 5000 cattle.

It was this stage in his life when the O crept back into Richard's name. Richard O' Donoghue died on October 11, 1878, in Potchefstrom, Zuid, African Republic of South Africa.

Donated 9/18/2016 by Larry O'Donoghue
  Retired, married, 3 children
Born in Boksbury Transvaal, South Africa, Lives in Benoni Gauteng, South Africa

Margaret Molloy

born 1818
Lynally Glebe, County Offaly, Ireland

MARGARET MOLLOY WAS A STRONG Catholic woman and in June 1840 she married Abraham Neville. Abraham Neville was the second son of William Neville, and a member of the Protestant Church of Ireland. They had four children, Joseph 1841, Maryann 1843, Anna 1844, and John 1847.

In 1850 Margaret and Abraham left Ireland for America for a better life and to purchase land. Land was very important to the Irish but Catholics couldn't buy land from the Protestants. Abraham knew his son could never inherit land in Ireland. Abraham knew he would not be able to inherit or purchase land from his father because he had married in the Catholic Church. His father could not give him the land, because of the Penal Laws. Abraham left his son John behind to secure their portion of William's land.

The family boarded the ship S.S. William D. Sewell and were at sea for about eight weeks with 240 other passengers and no doctor or running water. The ship was 141 feet long and 32 feet wide. The S.S. William D Sewell was a ship that hauled logs to England and to make more money the ship took people to America. Each family had a wooden birth for the family to sleep on, this was where the logs would be stored.

The ship landed in New York City, New York on April 11, 1850, and the family settled in Albany, New York. Margaret has another daughter and the family moves to Rawdon, Quebec, Canada. In 1857 a son,

James was born and Margaret is now 39 years old. In 1859 Margaret gives birth to twins, Herbert, and Margaret. Her son John finally arrived from Ireland to join the family in 1864, he was 17 years old.

Margaret's husband Abraham Neville died in Jan 1873 in Canada at the age of 74 years old and Margaret now 55 years old is left to care for nine children. Margaret decided to move the family to Greenbay, Wisconsin and her sons starts " Loggin" to make money. They want to own their own land and now must start to save.

In 1874 frontier land in Nebraska is up for sale and Margaret sends Joseph to York, Nebraska to purchase land for the family. Margaret buys 80 acres, Joseph and William buy 360 acres, John buys 160 acres and Joseph purchases another 160 acres. Margaret and her family arrive and work the land, but the first few years were very hard. In 1874, Nebraska, was devastated by swarms of grasshoppers that consumed everything.

In 1905 Margaret Molloy Neville died at the age of 87 years old. The 80 acres of land purchased by Margaret for $560 is today (2015) worth $800,000.

DONATED 7/16/2016 BY GR GREAT GRANDDAUGHTER
  BARBARA MCTYGUE SCANLON
BORN IN LEXINGTON, NEBRASKA, LIVES IN KANSAS CITY, MISSOURI
MARRIED, 4 CHILDREN, 8 GRANDCHILDREN
TAUGHT SCHOOL FOR 20 YEARS. ON THE BOARD OF THE KANSAS CITY
  IRISH CENTER

John McCarthy

born 5/28/1825
County Cork, Ireland

IN 1830 JOHN MCCARTHY EMIGRATED from Ireland to America with his parents at the age of 5 years from County Cork, Ireland. They landed in New York City, New York and settled in Oswego, New York. After, his public school, education, John served an apprenticeship in the Cooperage Trade. He learned the trade of shipbuilding in various branches in the Plants on Lake Erie. He traveled extensively on Ocean going vessels as a ships carpenter, visiting most of the principal ports of Eastern and Western Hemispheres.

In 1861 he married Miss Ellen Hopper of Albany, New York. In 1862 John established a shipbuilding plant on the Hudson River front, where he had a partnership with Benjamin Tilson. After 15 years, he dissolved his partnership with Benjamin Tilson. John and his brother James launched a similar enterprise on the property, which later became part of the Leigh Valley Railroad Company's freight yard system. 1890 John and his brother moved the plant to Hoboken, New Jersey and continued the ship building business.

In 1910 John decided to retire and sold his business to McWilliams Dry dock Company of Staten Island. John was a devoted member of St. Peter's Roman Catholic Church, New Jersey City, New Jersey, and at the time of his death, he was the oldest member of the parish. John McCarthy died at the age of 92 years on Jan 1, 1917 and is buried at Holy Name Cemetery, New Jersey City, New Jersey.

Donated 3/29/2016 by Gr Great Granddaughter
  Mary Schwarzenberger
Born in Jersey City, New Jersey, lives in Milford, New Jersey
Educator and Artist, 1 son

James Hughes

born 5/4/1871
Aughee, Dromore, Omagh, County Tyrone, Northern Ireland
Parents: Owen Hughes 1825-1897, Ellen Coll 1844-1879

JAMES HUGHES WAS ONE OF seven children born in the hilly village of Dromore, in County Tyrone, Northern Ireland. Dromore is Irish for hill or great ridge.

In 1890 James Hughes emigrated from Ireland to America, arriving in New York City, New York on Aug 12, 1890. With him was his childhood sweetheart Annie McCanny. Annie was born in 1871 and was also from County Tryone, Ireland. They marry in St Joseph's Catholic Church in New York City, New York and had Four children, with only two living to adulthood. James worked as a Trolly Conductor.

In 1903 James wife Annie McCanny Hughes died. When his wife died, James had to place his two young girls into the care of the Sisters of Charity of St. Vincent DePaul at St. Elizabeth Industrial School for girls. Usually children in this situation were given up for adoption.

Now James is working as much overtime as he can get to save money. James eventually saved a good amount of money and invested in real estate, owning "Klines" on the Union Square, which is a Bar/ Boarding House. He also invested in a Brownstone and several apartment buildings.

In 1907 James meets and marries Bridget McHale. Bridget McHale was born in 1879 and was from Kincon, County Mayo Ireland. They marry on Sept 25, 1907 and Bridget raised James two daughters. On

April 21, 1921 James and Bridget move into their waterfront home in Rockaway, Queens, New York.

In 1913 James purchases a large family Plot that buried forty-five people in Calvary Cemetery in Woodside, Queens, New York. James had his 1st wife and children exhumed from the original burial site and moved to the new family plot.

James Hughes died in New York City, New York in 1936. His wife Bridget McHale Hughes died on Jan 20, 1947 and they were buried together.

DONATED 5/8/2016 BY GREAT GRANDSON
  MICHAEL RICHARD SULLIVAN
BORN IN ASTORIA, QUEENS, NEW YORK. LIVES IN CONNECTICUT
SOCIAL WORKER, SINGLE

John Joseph Cunningham

born 12/1863
Castlenageeha, Kilcummin Parish, County Mayo Ireland
Parents: James Cunningham born in Cashel, County Mayo
died 1/3/1892;
Bridget Langan born 1833 – 1883

THE CUNNINGHAM'S WERE ORIGINALLY FROM Drumgore, County Armagh, Ulster, Northern Ireland. In the Late 1700's there were skirmishes with Catholics and Protestants, building up to The Battle called: "The Battle of the Diamond" where 30 Catholics were killed by Protestant Peep O'Day boys, later they became known as the "Orangemen". It was a precursor of the Orange Order or Orange Organization.

The Orange Order is a Protestant fraternal organization based primarily in Northern Ireland. It was founded in County Armagh in 1795, during a period of Protestant and Catholic conflict. It is headed, by the Grand Orange Lodge of Ireland, which was established in 1798. Its name is a tribute to the Dutch-born Protestant king William of Orange. The Order is best known for its yearly marches held on July 12. It does not accept Protestants married to Catholics.

The Peep O 'Day boys would wreck Catholic houses, posting written notice upon the door " To Hell or Connaught" on Catholic homes, telling them to flee or be subject to a worse fate. The Cunningham family left and settled into Cashel, County Mayo Ireland in 1795, where they found peace.

In 1880 at the age of 16 years old, John Cunningham left Ireland for Liverpool, England, from Liverpool, he immigrated to America. John landed in New York City, New York on June 14, 1880 on the Steamer S. S. Germanic. Once he landed, he made his way to Scranton Pennsylvania. Scranton was a center for Mayo Ireland immigrates. John went to work in the coal mines as a coal picker, then later became a Coal Miner. Coal mining was an extremely dirty and dangerous job. Miners were always worried about mine cave in's and explosions. Scranton, Pennsylvania was the center for Anthracite coal mining. Anthracite is the cleanest, hottest burning coal, making it extremely valuable.

John became a U.S. Citizen on Oct 6,1887. With all his hard work and saving' s he was able, to buy a home at 1329 Penn Ave. In Jan 1892 John's father died and a year later his mother died. John's siblings settle the estate and pay for passage to America. His sister Catherine married a Mr. Patrick Cook and they live at the home on 322 Pennsylvania Ave, across the street from John.

John meets and marries Rose Ratchford on Sept 26, 1894. Rose's father was from Ballina, Co Mayo Ireland, not far from the Cunningham home. John and Rose had six children. John is a strict father, pulling his sons out of school once they have learned to read and write, to work as coal pickers. They girls stay in school even go to college. John continues working in the mines and was able, to buy two more homes on Pennsylvania Ave. for his children for when they marry.

Unfortunately, like many coal miners, he succumbed to an illness related to mining. John Joseph Cunningham died on April 18, 1927 of acute Bronchitis from working in the mines. He died at the age of 63 years,

DONATED 3/2/2016 BY GREAT GRANDSON JOHN LOUGHNEY
BORN IN NEW JERSEY, LIVES IN CALIFORNIA, MARRIED, 2 CHILDREN

Denis Hamill

born 1790
Belfast, County Antrim, Northern Ireland
Parents: John Hamill, Margaret Unknown

DENIS HAMILL WAS 5'8" TALL, Catholic with black hair and grey eyes, who was a Weaver by trade. Denis had committed several highway robbery crimes in his early 20's. On March 24, 1812 at the age of 22 years, Denis was tried and found guilty of highway robbery and sentence to be hanged at Carrickfergus Assizes on April 24, 1812. His sentence was committed to life and he was transported to Australia, along with 218 other male convicts. They sailed from County Cork, Ireland on Dec 8,1813 on the ship Three Bees which arrived at Sydney Cove, New South Wales on May 6, 1814. Many convicts arrived in poor health and nine men Died aboard the ship during the voyage.

Denis's first job was working in the Government stores. In 1818 Denis met Maria Courtney Duffy, another Irish convict. Maria was born 1796 and was from Belfast, Ireland. She came over on the ship Friendship on Jan 14, 1818. On Sept 7, 1818 Denis and Maria asked for permission to marry from the Governor MacQuearie (a requirement for convicts). The request was granted and they married on Sept 28, 1818 in St. Philip's Church of England. Neither could read or right so they signed with and X.

Denis received his ticket to leave in 1819. (A ticket to leave allowed a convict to work on their own account within a specific district). Denis and Maria had four children.

In 1822 Denis and the family moved to the Windsor District on the Hawskesbury River. Denis tried his hand at farming. The Land and Stock Minster of 1822 shows Denis with a lease and a farm of 10 acres and he grew wheat, maize, potato and he had hogs.

Denis's wife, Maria Courtney Duffy Hamill died Feb 1828 at the age of 28 years in Wallis Plains. The children are 8,6,3,1. In 1832 there was flooding and loss of crops. By 1833 the area Denis lives in is lawless with Bushrangers everywhere. Denis moves the family to Sydney. The children all grow up and marry.

Denis Hamill died on Sept 17, 1860 at the age of 70 years old. He was living with his daughter Margaret at the time of his death.

Donated on 4/12/2016 by Gr Gr Great Granddaughter Rose Lee
Lives in Gundaldar, Queensland Australia
Artist, Graphic Engineer, Retired, 3 children, 4 grandchildren

Florence Harrington

born 1870
Milleen, Parish of Eyeries, Castlebere, County Cork
Ireland
Parents: Dan "Norr" Harrington, Johanna McCarthy

IT WAS DURING THE POST-FAMINE wave of emigration that members of the Loughman family from Hollyford, near Dundrum in County Tipperary, Ireland and the Harrington family from Eyeries, near Castletownbere in County Cork, made the way to the New World in the years 1888-1892 to eventually cross each other's paths in Butte, Montana and Colorado, and Utah. The journeys, both inter- and cross-continental, of brother and sister, Michael, and Molly Loughman, as well as Florence and Julia Harrington, another brother and sister, whom, as, a result of migration to the US and eventually return to Ireland, became inextricably linked with one another through the celebration of marriages to each other.

Florence Harrington born 1870, the same year, the Berehaven Mining Company, operated by the Puxley family of Dunboy, reopened the Allihies Copper Mines and installed a new 22- inch steam engine but little ore was produced in this period and the mine was finally abandoned in 1878. There was, however, little other employment in the beautiful but rugged and isolated landscape of Beara Peninsula in the 1880's except cattle farming and seine fishing. With the closing of the Allihies mines, many miners emigrated to the copper mines of North Michigan, Butte, Montana, and other Rocky Mountain mining camps in Utah and Colorado, and desert mining camps in Nevada and Arizona. In 1889 Florence Harrington emigrated from Ireland to America, arriving at Ellis Island, New York City, New York. He, was followed by his younger sister Julia.

Julia Harrington was born in 1873. She arrived on the ship S.S. Alaska on May 29,1893, having just turned 20 years old. Florence and Julia made their way to Butte Montana to work the silver mines. They then moved on to Colorado to work silver mins before the enterprise collapsed during the depression, during the Panic of 1893. This panic cased the Butte Montana Silver Mines to close.

In Colorado, Florence's younger sister Julia meets and married Michael Loughman. Michael Loughman was from County Tipperary Ireland. They marry in Utah in 1893 and moved to Aspin Colorado. Florence followed them later.

In 1903 Florence Harrington decided to return to Ireland. At the request, of Michael Loughman, Florence visits the Loughman Family in Hollyford, County Tipperary. At the Loughman home Florence meets Michael sister Mary (Molly) Loughman. They marry in 1905 and settle down and run the Loughman Farm at Ballytarsna, some 6 miles Northeast of the Rock of Cashel. It was more appealing to run a farm than return to the dangers of mining. 1917 Julia Harrington Loughman died in Morris Plains, New Jersey and was buried with her husband Michael in Holy Rood Cemetery, Morristown, New Jersey.

Thus, through the double marriage, the two families became inextricably linked The Harrington- Loughman connection and family reunion continue today. Last reunion was 2010 in Butte Montana.

DONATED ON 5/10/2016 BY GRAND NIECE DOLORES O'SHEA
BORN THURLES, COUNTY TIPPERARY, IRELAND
LIVES IN PORTUMNA, COUNTY GALWAY.

Elizabeth (Ellen) Harkins

born - 1794
County Londonderry, Northern Ireland
Parents John Harkins b- 1775, Margaret Harkins b-1775

JOHN AND MARGARET HARKINS WERE dairy farmers in County Londonderry known as Derry. Their daughter Elizabeth known as Ellen, was born in 1794. She was a milkmaid, and butter maker and washerwoman. She married a farmer with the family name of Moon and they had a daughter.

In 1794 Ellen was convicted of stealing bleached linen from the Bleach Green. Bleaching and drying were both used to be mainly outdoor activities, and they were closely related. The stretch of grass set aside for these jobs was called a bleaching-green or drying-ground whether you were spreading off-white linen on the ground to bleach in the sun, or just putting your laundry there to dry.

On sentencing her crime was known as a Bleach Green Robbery. It appears that her crime was stealing linen from a bleaching green. Fields in farms where the unbleached linen was laid for the final process of bleaching. The initial stages involved cow dung and milk.

Ellen described her occupation as milkmaid, butter maker, and washer, the latter presumably related to the linen bleaching process. Some farmers combined the related industries of dairying and linen bleaching due to the use of milk in the bleaching process.

Ellen was arrested for Grand Larceny in 1825. Her trial was on Mar 15 and she was given a life sentence and transported to Sydney, New

South Wales, Australia aboard the, ship S.S. Marine, which left from Limerick Ireland, leaving her husband and child back in Ireland. She was listed as 4 feet 11 inches tall, with freckles, brown hair, and hazel eyes and a Catholic.

On arriving in Sydney on July 10, 1825, along with 120 other female convicts. She was given a Master, Mr. Fotherley, whom she went to live with and worked in his home as his servant. On the 1825 convict muster, Ellen is reported as working in the female factory at Parramatta. Her name is recorded as Ellen Moore. This was a common mistake, errors occurred, many convicts having similar names. At Parramatta, women who were sent there worked hard spinning and weaving. They slept in the same premises.

Ellen met James Smith, who was an emancipated convict from County Fermaugh, Northern Ireland. He was the son of Andrew Smith and Jane Duggan Smith. James went on trial for burglary and felony and sentences to seven years. He was transported from Cork, Ireland on Aug 18, 1818 on board the ship S.S. Martha with 170 other convicts as well as 32 soldiers from the 67th and 87th Regiments. His ship arrived in Sydney on Dec 24, 1818 and the convicts were taken to Bringelly. James was placed into the servitude of Mr. Frederick Garling. On 1922 James applied for a Ticket to Leave and he received his certificate of Freedom in 1824.

Ellen and James applied to marry through the Convict Marriage Application process. The request was refused due to confusion with another convict with the afore mentioned name Ellen More.

Governors, encouraged marriage and family life in Australia, believing it served moral ends and brought stability to society. Various inducements, such as tickets of leave, pardons and assistance with establishing households were offered. A year later James and Ellen reapplied and the application was approved. Previously married convicts, were, allowed to marry after seven, year separation. Divorce was not possible in New South Wales, Australia until 1873.

James Smith and Ellen Harkins married in 1829 and they settled in the lower Hawkesbury near Windsor, one of the Governor Macquairie Towns. James became a famer on the Hawkesbury River north of Sydney. They had seven children, Ellen b-1827, James b-1828, John Joseph b-1829, Terrence b-1830, Ann Jane b-1832, Thomas b-1834, and Mary Jane b-1837. Ellen had to leave her other, child and first husband back in Ireland when she was sent to Australia, and at one time, sought help from a priest to try to locate her daughter but this was very unsuccessful. In 1840 Ellen was pardoned.

James Smith died Jan 11, 1857 and Elizabeth (Ellen) Harkins Smith died on Dec 26, 1862. They were buried at McGrath Hill, Sydney Australia.

Ellen's Gr Gr Great Grandson Malcolm Turnbull became Prime Minister of Australia in 2016.

DONATED 2/12/2017 BY GR GREAT GRANDDAUGHTER-IN-LAW
TERRY O'BRIEN
BORN AND LIVES IN SYDNEY, AUSTRALIA, TWO DAUGHTERS, MICHELLE, AND NATALIE
FORMER HIGH SCHOOL TEACHER AND PRINCIPAL

Honora Convey

born 1856
Swinford, County Mayo Ireland
Parents: Martin Convey, Winifred Mellet

HONORA CONVEY WAS BORN IN the small town of Swinford, pronounced Swineford, County Mayo, Ireland. The entire Convey family emigrated from Ireland to America for a better way of life. Landing in New York City, New York, they settled first in Osewego, New York. Then on to Albany, New York.

In 1880 Honora Convey met and married Luke Walsh, who was a Blacksmith from Kiltimagh, County Mayo, Ireland. They lived in Utica, New York. Honora Convey Walsh died in 1908 and her husband Luke Walsh died in 1909, Utica, New York.

DONATED 2/22/2016 BY HONORA'S GREAT GRANDDAUGHTER,
    KATE NELSON
BORN IN NEW HARTFORD, NEW YORK.
LIVES IN GARNER PENNSYLVANIA

Michael Sullivan

born 12/1887
Kennare, County Kerry Ireland
Parents: Michael (Gow) Sullivan 1845-1916,
Julia Doyle 1847-1931

MICHAEL SULLIVAN WAS BORN IN Clonee, Kennare, Country Kerry, in the south-west Region of Ireland, on the Atlantic Ocean. This is one of the most mountainous regions of Ireland.

Michael was the youngest of eight children. He emigrated from Ireland to America from Queenstown Ireland with his parents, two siblings and his little niece, to join his other three siblings, on Feb 6, 1897 in New York City, New York.

In New York Michael found a job working with the Teamsters driving horses and wagons. Later he attended night school and became a Police Officer for the New York Police Department. Moving up in ranks from a Patrolman in 1919 to a Sargent in 1923 to Lieutenant in 1929.

Michael used to take vacations every year in the Catskill Mountains of New York, as many young Irish Policemen and Fireman did. In the Catskills, he would stay at the John O'Keefe Mountain Spring House. It was here, at the Mount Spring House that Michael met Loretto Anna O'Keefe. She was the youngest of the John O'Keefe children. Loretto was born 1891 in DeBruce, Sullivan, New York. They were married in Sacred Heart Catholic on Oct 8, 1924 in DeBruce, Sullivan, New York. They had two children, Francis, and John, that they raised in Elmhurst, Queens, New York.

Michael Sullivan died in Feb 22, 1959 and was buried in St Peters Cemetery in Liberty, Sullivan New York. His wife Loretto O'Keefe Sullivan died Feb 25, 1977 in Binghamton, Broome, New York and was buried with her husband Michael.

DONATED 5/5/2016 BY GRANDSON MICHAEL RICHARD SULLIVAN
BORN IN ASTORIA, QUEENS NEW YORK, LIVES IN HAMDEN
   CONNECTICUT
SOCIAL WORKER, MARRIED 2 SONS

Martin Joseph Durkin

born 11/7/1863
Westport, County Mayo Ireland

MARTIN DURKIN WAS A CATTLEMAN in Westport, on the south-east coast of County, Mayo Ireland. In May 1894, after the loss of Cattle money at a fair, Martin went bankrupt, and then became a butcher. In 1889, he met and married his wife Mary Ann and they had five children.

In 1907 Martin and his family emigrated from Ireland to America arriving at Ellis Island, New York City, New York. They then traveled to Chicago, Illinois where Martin found employment as a Night Watchman in a store. On the 1910, Census, he and his family are listed as living at 1032 North Franklin St, Chicago, Illinois, where he rented an apartment. Martin Durkin applied for and became a Naturalized Citizen.

Martin Joseph Durkin died on June 27, 1923 of Chronic Nephritis. He was living at 1336 Roscoe St Chicago, Illinois. His wife MaryAnn Durkin died Aug 13, 1922 from Post Op Intestinal Obstruction.

DONATED 5/10/2016 BY GR GRANDDAUGHTER CAROL SPRY
BORN IN CHICAGO ILLINOIS, LIVES IN NEW JERSEY
SINGLE, 4 CHILDREN, 5 GRANDCHILDREN

Margaret Swanton

born 12/15/1834
SkIibereen, County Cork Ireland
Parents: Richard Swanton, Elizabeth O'Connell

MARGARET SWANTON MET AND MARRIED George Swanton (No relation) on Feb 24, 1852 in the Registration District of Skibereen, County Cork Ireland.

Skibereen was the hardest hit area during the Great Famine. George Swanton was born in East Skull, Cork in 1830. They immigrated to Hamilton Lake Ontario, Canada in 1853. At this, time the Hamilton Rail Lines, were being built by Irish labor. Cholera arrived with the immigrants of 1854, and hundreds of local, residents fled the town. Margaret and George moved to Brunt River, Ontario, Canada and by 1859, Margaret and George owned a 50-acre farm near Burnt River, Ontario, growing wheat, peas, turnips, and potatoes. Between, 1854 and 1875, they had ten children: William, Richard, Mary Jane, Sarah Ann, Elizabeth, George, John, Margaret, James, and Patience. By 1881 Margaret's widowed Mother, Elizabeth Swanton, also resided with them.

In 1892 the family moved to Rosewood, Manitoba Canada where Margaret was a was a dressmaker. The following year Margaret was a widow when George died on Jan 8, 1893 in a lunatic asylum in Manitoba. By 1901 Margaret had returned to the Ontario homestead, living with a British home child, Elizabeth Caley, who helped Margaret douse a house fire with snow on Christmas Eve between 1904-1907. After 1911,

Margaret and George Swanton returned to Manitoba, where she died on Feb 2, 1923. Margaret and George were buried in Rosewood Cemetery.

Donated 3/23/2016 by Great Granddaughter Pat Javor.
Born in Toronto, Ontario, married, 1 daughter
Retired Communication Consultant

James Joseph Kearney

born 1/26/1889
Cloona, Westport, County Mayo Ireland

JAMES JOSEPH KEARNEY WAS THE eldest of ten children to Patrick Kearney and Mary Conway that lived in Cloona, Westport, County Mayo. Cloona is in the remote part of west Mayo. In the 1860's it was a thriving Woollen Industry, making tweeds and shawls.

James emigrated from Ireland to America aboard the ship S.S. Cedric, arriving at Ellis Island, New York on Aug 31, 1912. He found work with Sheffield Farms, at 524 West 57th St, New York, where he worked as a home delivery milkman, for 36 years. He served in the Armed Forces in WWI.

James married Katherine (Kitty) Loughnane on Aug 12, 1919 in Bronx, New York. Kitty Loughnane was born Dec 1887 in Freakle, County Clare, Ireland, the daughter of Patrick Loughnane and Anne Minoque Loughnane. They had one daughter, Margaret Mary, and one son, James Joseph Jr.

James became a Naturalized Citizen of the United States. James and his family lived in New York at the time of the building of the Empire State Building and the Chrysler Building. In 1944 the family lived at 47-50 98th Place, Corova, Queens New York.

James Kearney died Jan 11, 1949 in Chicago Illinois. His wife Katherine Loughnane Kearney died Dec 30, 1958. They were buried together in Long Island National Cemetery, Farmingdale, Suffolk, New York.

58 | Clare Ann Conway

Donated 3/2/2016 by Grandson Patrick (Paddy) Savage
Lives in Chicago Illinois, married 3 children, 2 grandchildren
Retired Head Cross County and Track and Field Coach, at DePaul University

Thomas Barry Moriarty M. D. R.A.M.

born 5/26/1813
Bruff, County Limerick Ireland
Parents: James Moriarty 1787-1868 Killmallock,
Limerick; Mary Catherine Bridget Barry 1797-1861
Bruff, Limerick

THOMAS MORIARTY WAS BORN IN Bruff, a town in East Limerick, in the Midwest of Ireland. December 1863, Thomas Moriarty joined the Army and went to West Africa, West African Brigade 1st BNT. He also served in England and India. He met Margaret McCarthy and they married on Nov 26, 1868 in St. Patrick's Church in Cork Ireland. Margaret McCarthy was born in 1832 in Limerick Ireland. Thomas and Margaret had three daughters.

Thomas was appointed Surgeon Major in 1876 to the British Army and he served the Peshawar Column in the 81st Regiment against Jowaki Afridi in Pakistan in 1877- 1878. Thomas retired Jan31,1881 with half pay and the rank of Brigadier Surgeon. 1884- 1910 Thomas was Medical Officer to a Female Prison in Cork Ireland. Thomas Moriarty died Oct 14, 1912 and buried at St. Patrick Hill. Cork Ireland. His wife Margaret McCarthy Moriarty died in 1919 in Cork Ireland.

DONATED 3/14/2016 BY MARY JANE KIRBY
BORN IN MELBOURNE, VICTORIA, AUSTRALIA, LIVES IN COOKATOO, A SUBURB OF MELBOURNE
RETIRED RECEPTIONIST FOR A DOCTOR'S OFFICE, MARRIED, 2 SONS

Ellen McGovern

born 1862
County Meath, Ireland

ELLEN MCGOVERN WAS BORN IN County Meath, which is on the Mid-East coast of Ireland. Ellen McGovern emigrated from Ireland to America with her parents at the age of 3 years old and they arrived at New York City, New York. Years later the family moved to Newark, New Jersey, where Ellen worked in a factory and here she met James Kelaher. James Kelaher was born on April 21, 1847 from Mohill Parish, County Leitrim, Ireland, which is a border county to Northern Ireland.

Ellen and James married on June 16, 1879 in St. John's Church, Newark, New Jersey. Then they moved to Haverhill, Massachusetts where James found work in a shoe factory. They had four children, all died of Diphtheria just two weeks apart. Ellen gave birth to another child on the same day as losing two of her children. She went on to have five more children and then the family moved to Salem, Mass.

Now her husband James had a heart problem that caused him to pass out and appear to have died. Ellen started to prepare a turkey and other foods for his wake on at least two occasions and on both occasions James revived. When James actually did die, Ellen did not have enough money for the extra food for his wake.

James Kelaher died on Jan 15, 1922. Ellen McGovern Kelaher died on Dec 6, 1943. At the time, she died, Ellen McGovern Kelaher was living with her daughter in Hyde Park, Mass.

Donated 4/2/2016 by Great Granddaughter
  Kathy Dewey McKinnon
Born in Quincy Mass., lives in West Boylston Mass.
Married, 1 son, 1 daughter, 2 grandchildren
Worked as an Office Administrator in a medical setting

Hugh Beggan

born 9/5/1881
Rahard, Old Castle, County Meath Ireland
Parents: James Beggan 1815-1892,
Bridget Farrelly 1850-1901

HUGH BEGGAN WAS ONE OF five children. On March, 1920 he married Anna Maria Hetherton and they had six children. Anna Maria was from Coronagh, Virginia, County Cavan Ireland.

In 1927, Hugh Beggan emigrated from Ireland to Canada aboard the ship S.S. Minnedosa, arriving St. John Ontario on March 12, 1927. He moved to Canada to find and job and establish a new home for his family. Hugh continued onto South Algona, Ontario Canada, where he found work as a farmer on the Jeremiah Dunning farm. The job came with a farmhouse to live in. Four months later he sent for his wife and children.

Anna Maria Beggan and her sons James, Patrick Joseph, and daughter Bridget Mary boarded the ship S.S. Mont Royal on Oct 27, 1927 that departed from Cobh Ireland. She met her husband in Renfrew Ontario and they took up residency in Douglas Ontario for a couple of years.

During the Depression 1933 they moved to a new farm and their son Tom was born. Anna Maria needed to go to the hospital for an operation and asked neighbors Tom and Lizzy O'Connor to watch their 6- month old son Tom. Hugh was looking after the other children when a house fire broke out and the house burnt to the ground. Hugh took the children to live with the family Kitts, who owned a general store in Cormac, Ontario.

Anna Maria had to be transferred to a Kingston Hospital and later to a specialty hospital in Woodstock. Anna would never return home. In 1936, Hugh succumbed to pneumonia and died on Feb 5, 1936 in the Victoria Hospital in Renfrew. He was buried at St Ann's Cemetery in Cormac Ontario, Canada.

The children first went to live with Father George and Mrs. Jack Kitts to be cared for. Eventually all seven children when to seven different generous and kind homes in the Cormac area.

Anna Maria was never to return home. She died in 1946 in Woodstock Ontario and was buried with her husband. The Beggan Family were held in high regards by the local Community.

DONATED 6/13/2016 BY GREAT GRANDSON DAVID BEGGAN LUCAS BORN IN EAST TORONTO CANADA, LIVED IN HOLDEN, MASSACHUSETTS MARRIED, 2 CHILDREN, 1 GRANDDAUGHTER.

Mary Kelly

born 1803
Drumshanbo, County Leitrim Ireland
Parents: John Kelly b-1773, Margaret Kelly b-1774

MARY KELLY WAS BORN IN Drumshanbo, County Leitrim, Ireland. Drumshanbo is (Irish) for Ridge of the Old Huts. It is a small town situated in the heart of County Leitrim, Ireland. Drumshanbo has three churches and a convent. St. John's Church of Ireland built in 1829, St. Patrick's Roman Catholic Church built in 1845, the Metholdis Church built 1760's, and the Poor Clare Convent was built in 1860.

Mary met John McQueeny, who was from the same town and they married and had eight children: Margaret b-1828, Ann b-1829, Bridget b-1831, Mary B-1832, Catherine b-1834, Eliza b-1836, Alice b--1842 and John b-1844.

John and Mary were very poor and they ended up with their children going to and residing in the Workhouse in Drumshanbo. The Workhouse was built in 1840 and was declared fit for admission of paupers on July 1, 1842. This was a very hard time with the potato famine and a young family to care for with no money. John and Mary decided to send their daughters, overseas, and give them new lives.

The eldest daughters Margaret and Ann left Ireland and immigrated to America in 1846. The next two daughters, Bridget and Mary were sent to Australia as part of the Earl Grey program.

They went to England and boarded the ship S.S. Lady Peel out of Plymouth on March 14,1849. The girls arrived in Sydney, Australia on

July 6,1849 as Famine Orphans. Neither Bridget or Mary could read or write. From Sydney, they made their way to Brisbane, where Bridget found work as a housemaid. Bridget McQuinney married a William Bowden, who was a convict from England, on Dec 26,1849. Mary married James Cash a convict from England.

John McQueeny passed away in 1854 and was buried at the Drumshanbo Famine Cemetery which is just on the outskirts of the city. This was a, paupers grave with no headstone. The cemetery entrance is through the old gate of the Drumshanbo Famine Graveyard, there are just stone walls enclosing areas of beautiful Irish green grass, and some 500 victims of the Great Famine are buried here. A rosary hangs from a tree in the center of the cemetery.

In 1855, after John died, Mary left Ireland with her children Catherine age 23, Elizabeth age 19, Alice age 17 and John age 15, and boarded the ship S.S. Robert Small for Brisbane, Australia. Mary's son-in-law, James Chase sponsored them to come to Australia. James paid Thirty-Two pounds, sterling for their passage.

Mary's son-in-law James Cash was born in Birmingham England in 1804. He was convicted for armed theft of leather from Thomas Whitehouse in England and sentenced to seven years and transported to Australia. His trade and occupation was Pressure Hinge Dresser and fitter. James received his letter of freedom on Jan 24,1842.

Mary Kelly McQueeny died May 25,1870 at the age of 67 years old of Bronchitis and was buried at Lutwyche Cemetery in Brisbane, Queensland, Australia. And she was buried with her husband John Cash, Section RC1, Section16, Grave 62.

DONATED 2/27/2017 BY GR GR GREAT GRANDDAUGHTER
   JENNIFER ROOKS
BORN IN DALBY, QUEENSLAND, AUSTRALIA
MARRIED, 3 SONS, 3 GRANDCHILDREN, RETIRED FROM EDUCATION

Helen Browne

born 9/6/1881
Swinford, County Mayo Ireland
Parents: Denis Browne 1844-1924,
Bridget McNicholas 1846-1904

HELEN BROWNE WAS ONE OF twelve children. She emigrated from Ireland to America at the age of 16, in 1897 with her brother Frank. All but one of her Siblings immigrated to America, her brother Joseph stayed in Ireland. They all settled in Jersey City, New Jersey, and she worked as a domestic. In 1906 Helen did return to Ireland to visit her Father.

When she came back to New Jersey she worked for the Waterman Pen Company. Helen had many suitors but when she met Herman Henrich Kirchner, she knew he was the one she would marry. Herman Henrich Kirchner was an immigrant born Sept 5, 1882 from Menslage, Lower Saxony, Germany. He was the son of Herman Bernhart Kirchner and Marie Adelheid Lanfer, and was a Motorman for the Electric Railroad. Helen and Herman married in 1915 at Our Lady of Grace Church in Hoboken, New Jersey, when Helen was 34 years old. They had three children, Muriel, Helen, and Henry.

Neither Muriel or Henry had children. Helen married Frank J Sullivan and had two children. Helen Browne Kirchner died on June 25, 1954 in Jersey City, New Jersey at the age of 72 years. Helen's husband Herman Kirchner died on March 19, 1957 at the age of 74 years and they were married for 39 years.

Clare Ann Conway

Donated 3/10/2016 by Granddaughter Susan DeBarba
Born Jersey City, New Jersey, Lives in Hazlet, New Jersey
Married, 4 stepchildren, 7 grandchildren

Thomas Francis Flaherty

born 12/11/1838
County Galway, Ireland
Parents: James Flaherty, Margaret Coyne

THOMAS FLAHERTY EMIGRATED FROM IRELAND to America in the Spring of 1861 and landed in the Port of South Boston, Massachusetts. He continued to travel up to Lewiston, Maine, where Thomas found work on the Androscoggin Railroad where he stayed working for one year. He then traveled to New Hampshire where he found work on the Grand Trunk Railroad and worked here for one year.

Thomas then traveled to Washington, D.C and found work for the Government. Thomas worked for the Union Army baking their bread, during the Civil War.

It was here in Washington D.C. Thomas met Margaret Gavin. They married in 1864 when he was 25 years old. Thomas and Margaret went on to have eleven children. Their first daughter Margaret was born in Feb 1865 in Washington D.C. They lived in Washington before and after the assignation of President Abraham Lincoln.

The city was under Martial Law and everyone was confined to their home. They where not allowed out of their homes to even buy food. In 1867 the family moved to Gorham New Hampshire, were their ten children were all born on Promenade St. in Gorham. In Gorham, Thomas was the foreman on the Railroad from Shelburne to Berlin New Hampshire.

Thomas F Flaherty died on March 30, 1913 in Gorham New Hampshire at the age of 74 years and was buried in Holy Family Cemetery, Gorham N.H.

This story was obtained from letters written by Thomas youngest daughter, Annie Elizabeth Flaherty, to her niece Margaret Leone Flaherty. Margaret L Flaherty shared the letters with Pauline Maht Wilson.

DONATED 6/12/2016 BY GREAT GRANDDAUGHTER
  PAULINE MAHT WILSON
BORN PORTLAND MAINE, LIVES IN KENNEBUNK MAINE
MARRIED, RETIRED MEDICAL ASSISTANT IN A WALK-IN CLINIC

Patrick McHugh

born 1889
Meenamullen Rd. Killeter, County Tyrone, Northern Ireland

PATRICK MCHUGH WAS A HUMBLE farmer. In 1928 Patrick took advantage of the "Passage Paid" system to Canada, which encourage settlers to Canada. The Passage was $1. He left Ireland and landed first in Halifax, Nova Scotia, Canada. From here he moved on to Toronto Canada.

In 1933, Patrick married Elizabeth Hasson, whom he from knew back in Ireland. Elizabeth was born in 1905 in Feeney, County Derry Ireland. On July 1927, she arrived in Quebec, Canada on the ship S.S. Andrania. Elizabeth was a housekeeper. When she arrived in Quebec, Elizabeth knew no one and only had $5 in her pocket. She was bound to go on to a women's refuge in Toronto, Canada. It took several days to go from Quebec to Toronto, traveling thru twisting roads through mountains and lakes.

Patrick and Elizabeth lived in what was called, Cabbage Town, a suburb of Toronto. This was called Cabbage Town because the Irish dug up their front yards and planted vegetable gardens. They lived in bitterly cold winters and blistering hot summers in Cabbage Town.

In 1930 the Depression came and Patrick and Elizabeth decided to go back home to Ireland, and return to Patrick's home. Here there is no electricity or running water. It is a clay floor and the nearest village is a long walk away. The view from every window is the same, heather covered hills and no other houses to be seen. Patrick and Elizabeth never talk about their life in Canada. Here Patrick farmed and they have four lovely children, all born at home.

Later in life Elizabeth moved to England to be with her daughter and Granddaughter. Patrick stays behind in Killeter, County Tyrone Ireland and never left. He died alone on the hill, an old man.

Donated 5/29/12016 by Granddaughter Noelene McGuire
Born in Burmingham, England,
works in the automotive market. Married.

John S Sullivan

Born 12/16/1846
Cloherance, County Kerry Ireland
Parents: John Sullivan, Mary Sullivan

JOHN S SULLIVAN SPENT HIS childhood years doing farm work and chores and he also, gained a good common education in school. Later in life he met and married Mary Sullivan and they have five children, four that lived. Mary Sullivan was born June 5, 1847 and was from Ardnacluggin, Kitcatherine Eyeries, Parish, County Cork.

John had wanted to travel and start a new life for himself and his family. In 1880 John immigrated to America by himself, landing in New York City, New York. From New York, he continued, on to Michigan, doing manual labor jobs. He traveled on to California, but this was not at all to his liking so in 1884 John migrated on to Latah, Idaho where he decided to settle down and live. John purchased 80 acres of land in Latah County that he paid $58 an acre for. Then he put his farming kills and labor practices into making a very fertile farm, where he even built his own farm house. John had purchased one of the finest pieces of agriculture in the entire County of Latah and had become a very prosperous farmer. In 1886, John had saved enough money to send for his wife and children to come join him.

In 1892 John purchased two hundred and twelve acres more of land. With this land he planted and raised ten thousand bushels of grain in one year. In 1893 there were terrible rains and flooding, this year John lost the entire crop. By 1896 John bought another 160 acres and his hard work paid off. His land was now improved with several buildings added. John now raised cattle, hogs and horses. He was a very prosperous landowner and was a great example for all the neighboring countrymen to know.

John S. Sullivan died Dec 1928 and his wife Mary died 1918 in Latch County Idaho. They were buried at St. Mary the Immaculate Cemetery in Genesee, Latah, County, Idaho.

Donated 6/2/2016 by Gr Granddaughter
    Jane Cowley Von Bothmer.
Born in Idaho, lives in San Francisco, married.
Board member of Hamilton Family Center

Mary Molly

born 1881
Falls Road, Belfast, Northern Ireland
Parents: William Henry Molly 1858-1886,
Roseann Britton 1858-1935

WILLIAM HENRY MOLLY WAS FROM Gifford, County Down, Northern Ireland, which is on the northeast coast of Ireland. Roseann Britton was from Belfast Northern Ireland. William Molly was a hackler, preparing the Flax before it was spun. In this linen mill, he met his wife Roseann Britton, who was a weaver. Roseann and William married and had two girls, Mary, and Annie Molly.

William Henry had decided to take the family to live in Kilburnie, Ayrshire Scotland. On the boat ride, over to Scotland, Henry got sick, mostly likely Tuberculosis (TB) and he never recovered. By 1886 the Family was back in Belfast and William Henry had died, leaving his wife Roseann, a widow with two small girls. Roseann was unable to work and look after the girls so they were sent to the nuns in Whitefield (outside the city) where they received a good education.

In 1893 Roseann meets and remarries a James McManus and the girls returned home to Belfast. Roseann then had three children with James McManus, Francis, Clara and Nelly. She is very busy with the younger children to look after. As the Mary and Annie get older they plan to leave home. Annie went and trained as a seamstress. Mary went to work as a servant for a Pawnbroker in the Pottinger area of Belfast. Roseann had started to take in Lodgers.

In 1901 a Joseph Kerr had come to stay at Roseann's home. He was a committed Marxist and he worked in the Mills as a flax dresser. Joseph Kerr was a well educated man. He lived with Roseann's family in cramped conditions. By 1905 Mary had fallen for him and they married. Mary and Joseph moved to their own home on Abyssinia St. They live in Belfast and have five children, Annie, Molly, Joe, George, and Jimmy.

In this time, attempts were going on to strengthen the trade union movement in the Mills. There was a strike that cased hardship to Joseph. There was also a lot of Ant- Catholic feelings and Joseph found it very difficult to find work.

In Belfast, opposition to the government Plans for Home Rule for Ireland had led to the formation of the Ulster Volunteers and Armed Militia on both sides of the political divide.

Mary had a cousins John McHenry, who was a full time official of the National Union of Seamen and he had a job as a fireman on the Ferries between Scotland and Belfast. In 1915 John suggested that Mary and her family should come to live with him in Saltcoasts in Scotland. Which they do, they move to Saltcoats by the sea but they still battle prejudice.

Saltcoats is also the home for what was known as " Dynamite" a huge explosive Works, which was set up by Alfred Noble, the inventor of dynamite. The work well paid and with outbreak of the First World War, business was booming and jobs were plentiful but it was also very dangerous. It was here Joseph went to work making armaments. They move into a tenement flat and the neighbors protest to the building owner to have the Irish family evicted. The owner goes to see Mary and sees she keeps the flat clean and where she is the only one paying rent on time the owner says he won't evict her. After a time, Mary makes friends with the neighbors. She joins the local labor party. Although now the neighbors are not her only problem, on the outbreak of WWI, no one, could to get in contact with her sister Annie.

With the end of the WWI, there is less work at the "Dynamite and Mary decides she doesn't want her sons working at this dangerous place and they move back to Belfast Ireland. 1920, following what was known as the Fourth Home Rule Bill, was a warning of the dangers of the Sinn Fein which would have an inflammatory effect in the city. 5,000 Catholics working in the shipyard were attached and forced to leave their jobs. There was gunfire in the area where Mary and her family lived. Men dressed like soldiers took every man into the street, lined them up and every other man was shot to death. Joseph was lucky but they could no long stay in Ireland. They fled to Scotland. They are a family of eight in a single room. Joseph could no longer find work but his daughters, Molly and Annie get work in the garment factory.

At the end of WWII in 1940 Joseph Kerr died and Mary went back to Belfast. Mary planned to move to Scotland to be with her daughter, she went to visit and died at the daughter's home. Mary Molloy Kerr died in 1951 in Glasgow Scotland.

DONATED 5/12/2016 BY GREAT GRANDDAUGHTER CLAIRE MELVIN
BORN IN INVERNESS SCOTLAND, LIVES IN SOUTH LONDON
PUBLISHER FOR A MIDDLE EAST LAW FIRM
MARRIED, 2 CHILDREN

Ann Jane Marks

born 4/16/1829
Magherafelt, County Londonderry, Northern Ireland
Parents: William Marks, Ann Scott

ANN JANE MARKS WAS BORN in Magherafelt, a small town in Londonderry. Ann Jane Marks left Ireland at the age of 18 years old with her three sisters, Ellen, Margaret and Mary and departed from Liverpool England aboard the ship S.S. St Lawrence, to America and arrived in Philadelphia, Pennsylvania on May 26, 1845. Shortly after they arrive in Philadelphia, Ann Jane got separated from her sisters and never saw them again.

In Philadelphia, Ann met James Arment Lane. James Lane was born in July 25, 1822 from Lancaster, Pennsylvania and was a shoemaker. They married on March 14, 1849 in Harrisburg, Dauphin County, Pennsylvania and then moved to Indiana and then on to Iowa and they raised eight children.

In 1869 James had a homestead of 80 acres of Government land. Later he owned 200 acres of land in Silver and Pilot Townships. Here Ann Jane is a beloved member of the Methodist Church.

Ann Jane Marks Lane died on April 7, 1889 and her husband James Arment Lane died on Jan 19, 1901. They are buried together in Cherokee, Cherokee, Iowa.

DONATED 4/18/2016 BY GREAT NIECE SHERI LAMELE
BORN IN OAK PARK, ILLINOIS, LIVES IN ST. LOUIS, MISSOURI
RETIRED, 1 CHILD

Yehuda Maisha Shillman

born 1858
Krustpils (previously Kreutzberg) Vitebsk Latvia
Courland Province of Latvia
Parents: Dr. Isaac Schillman d-1912 Traverse City,
Michigan;
Pessa Benson d-1902 Traverse City, Michigan

YEHUDA MAISHA SHILLMAN (JULIUS MAURICE in English) was a Jewish traveling Pedlar and dealer as well as a grocer. He married Ada Mirrelson. Ada was born in 1858, and was the daughter of Yehuda Leib and Brayna Mirrelson, in Courland, then a province of Latvia, she was a Midwife.

The Jewish immigrant often arrived in Ireland with nothing, having left their, professions and trades behind them in the old country. Some came over to family already living in Ireland. They embraced Ireland as their new country. They worked hard as peddlers, cigarette makers, salesmen and hawkers.

In 1882, Yehuda and his wife crossed the Baltic Sea, sailed down the North Sea, around the English Channel and finally disembarked in Cobh Harbor, Cork Ireland. They first settled in 5, East Village, Cork and then moved to No:1 Mardyke Villas where their first four children were born; Tilly b-1883, Louis b-3/1884, Gerty b-1886, and Annie b-1888.

In 1892 the Shillmans moved to Dublin, where they had another four children; Barney (Bernard) b-Dec 19, 1892, Bertha b-Feb 19, 1894, Gracie b-July 8, 1896 and youngest Fanny b-Nov 29, 1901.

On Rosh Hashanah, the Jewish New Year, (Sept-Oct) Yehuda and Ada with the family would sit down to a lavish table laden with food. Yehuda would do a blessing over the wine, then do a ritual hand-washing and partake in Challah (bread) which would be baked in a rounded shape, and they ate it with lots of honey. Their meal would start with various fishes, recipes from "der Heim" the home. Gelfilter fish boiled with a carrot on top, Danish herring, chopped herring, pickled and potted herring and pickled cucumbers, followed by chicken soup and Kneidlach (a kind of dumpling), Tzimmes (a dish of meat, cooked slowly and prunes and lots of honey) Roasted Chicken and roasted potatoes. Taiglach, a sort of, sticky very sweet biscuit, would also be on their table. Also, apples dipped in honey. Honey signifies a sweet New Year. On the 2nd night of Rosh Hashanah they would eat "new fruit", something just coming into season. Yehuda and Ada were very religious and went to Shul (Synagogue) to pray on Shabbos (Saturday) mornings.

Yehuda Maisha was naturalized on Sept 18, 1902 and his family lived in Warren Street and later at 33 Victoria Street, South Circular Road district, (SCR) which was fast becoming home to all the Jews who were coming to Ireland in droves from Lituavia and Latvia. (Known as "The Litvaks"). The SCR had a street called Clanbrassil Street and this was where the Jewish Butcheries, book shops, Dairy shops and haberdashery shops all thrived.

Yehuda Maisha Shillman was a very proud member of the "Lodge". He was the founder and past noble master of the Dublin Lodge. He has two sisters and one brother. One sister and her husband moved to Ireland for 20 years and the older brother and sister went to America.

Ada Mirrelson Shillman was always seen around Dublin with her black hat, dress and cape. She was a short and rather stout woman with a heart of gold. She was a tower of strength and loved by all. Ada could not read or write English but could speak it fluently with her Yiddish accent.

She was known as Nurse Shillman to the community and Grandma Shillman to her family. Ada Mirrelson Shillman had three brothers and a sister. Her sister went to America, one brother went to Ireland and her two brothers stayed in the old country. They kept in contact with one another but suddenly no more letters came to Ireland from the brothers and they were presumed to have perished.

Ada became a very famous midwife both in Cork and later in Dublin. She was highly thought of and known to be a "Woman of Worth". She worked alongside the famous Dr Bethel Solomons, the Master of the Rotunda Maturnity Hospital. Ada would often wait a few months to go register the babie's births, and she would registered them all on the same day, so that many children had Birthdays, which were not, their actual, the day of their birth. Her birth book, in her own handwriting, along with a lot of Shillman memorabilia and photographs are on display to this day, in the Dublin Jewish Museum, at 3 Walworth Road.

Yehuda Maisha Shillman died of Nephrites on Aug 2, 1920 and his wife Ada Mirrelson Shillman died Oct 11, 1933 of Pneumonia and Heart Failure. Both Yehuda Maisha Shillman and his wife Ada Mirrelson Shillman died in Dublin, Ireland and are buried together in the Dublin Jewish Cemetery, Dolphin's Barn.

DONATED BY 9/25/2016 GREAT GRANDDAUGHTER ANN LAPEDUS BREST BORN DUBLIN IRELAND, LIVES IN SANDTON (JOHANNESBURG AREA),
  SOUTH AFRICA
PHOTOGRAPHER, PUBLISHED AUTHOR, GENEALOGIST
DIVORCED MOTHER OF 2 CHILDREN, ANGELA, AND GREGORY BREST

John Hoban

born 1859
Castlebar, County Mayo, Ireland
Parent: Thady Hoban

JOHN HOBAN WAS A HERDSMAN in the market town of Castlebar, which is the largest town in County Mayo Ireland. He met Mary McDonnell and they married in Westport, County Mayo, on Feb 27, 1887. Mary was born on Oct 29, 1865 in Ballycastle, County Mayo, which is four hours from Castlebar. She was the daughter of Dominic McDonnell and Honoria Clifford.

In 1901, they lived at Glenummera, Erriff, County Mayo Ireland. John and Mary had six children and four of their children went to America. Mary raised her children and was a housewife.

DONATED 3/2/ 2016 BY GREAT GRANDDAUGHTER MAUREEN LEHNER
BORN IN CHICAGO, ILLINOIS, LIVES IN NEW LENOX, ILLINOIS
MARRIED, 3 CHILDREN, 7 GRANDCHILDREN

Oliver Nash Moriarty Lt. Col.

born 11/18/1882
Minard, County Kerry, Ireland
Parents: John Battesworth Moriarty 1847-1982,
Sarah Jemina Moriarty 1855-1931

IN 1901 OLIVER MORIARTY LIVED at the Wood Quay, Dublin, Ireland. From 1910-1950 Oliver was in the Great Britain, Royal Aero Club Aviators. Oliver met Georgina Elsie Moore while in Dublin. Georgina Moore was born on May 6, 1886 and was the daughter of William George Moore and Sarah Emily Sadlier. They lived at 25 Birkley Road, Dublin Ireland. Oliver and Georgina married on March 1919 and had two children, one son and one daughter.

In WWI Oliver was with the British Army, Royal Garrison Artillery. April 2,1911, they lived at Carrickfergus Urban, Antrim, Northern Ireland.

Oliver's wife Georgina Moore Moriarty died June 1, 1974 in Witshire, England and Oliver Moriarty died on Sept 1974 in Trowbridge, Witshire, England.

DONATED 3/4/2016 BY MARY JANE KIRBY
BORN IN MELBOURNE, VICTORIA, AUSTRALIA,
    LIVES IN COCKATOO, MELBOURNE
MARRIED, 2 SONS, RETIRED

William Watson

born 5/25/1812
Lurgan, County Armagh, Northern Ireland
Parents: Robert Watson 1776-1848,
Ann Emerson 1782-1831

IN NORTHERN IRELAND, THE WATSON Family owned a Linen Factory in Lurgan, County Armagh, Northern Ireland. The town is near the southern shore of the Lough Neagh and in the north-eastern corner of the county. Lurgan is about 18 miles south-west of Belfast. The Watson's were Protestant and had six children. Their son William was also a merchant in the family business.

William Watson married Maria Campbell on Jan 29, 1838 in Belfast Antrim, Northern Ireland. Maria Campbell was born on March 3, 1817 and was from Belfast. In 1847 William, his wife Maria and their three children emigrated from Ireland to America, landing in New York City, New York.

William moved to America to create a new Linen Market for his family and he became a very wealthy merchant. William and Maria had six children, three of whom were born in New York. In Aug 22, 1860, the Watson's resided in Westchester, Westchester, New York.

On several occasions, William did return to Ireland for visits. He applied for New York Alien Deposition of Intent to become a U.S. Citizen on May 3, 1835 and paid A fee of $1.00.

William Watson died on Sept 28, 1877 at the age of 66 years old. His wife Maria Campbell Watson died on July29, 1894. They are buried at Woodlawn Cemetery, Bronx, Bronx County, New York.

Donated on 3/31/2016 by Great Grandson David Watson Born in New York, Lives in New York, married

Delia Bridget Coleman

born 6/13/1880
Sraheen, Aghagower, County Mayo Ireland
Parents: Martin Coleman 1851-1892,
Anne O'Malley 1857-1945

DELIA COLEMAN WAS ONE OF seven children of Martin and Anne Coleman. They lived in the tiny village of Aghagower. A large part of the population of Aghagower was lost in the Great Famine. This village, was visited by St. Patrick on his way to Croagh Patrick.

At the age of 16 years, Delia married William Malone, who was a Tailor and the son of Neal Malone and Alice Sheridan. William and Delia left Ireland and immigrated to America in 1898 arriving in New York City, New York. They continued, on and settled in Chicago, Illinois where William found work as a Tailor in a Department Store. In 1940, their address was 2415R Geneva Terr, Chicago, Illinois. They had six children. William Malone died in 1953 and Delia Coleman Malone died 1959.

DONATED 3/2/2016 BY GREAT NEPHEW JAMES COLEMAN
BORN IN CHICAGO ILLINOIS, LIVES IN INVERNESS, ILLINOIS,
SOLD SCHOOL CLASS RINGS, DID MARKETING FOR MEDICAL AFFILIATED ASSOC.
MARRIED, 3 DAUGHTERS, 4 GRANDCHILDREN

Joseph Redmond

born 1898
Kilbranish, County Carlow, Ireland
Parents: Andrew Redmond 1865-1943,
Ann Cobbe 1865-1949

JOSEPH REDMOND MET CATHERINE O'BOYLE in Castlebar, County Mayo, Ireland. Catherine attended the Fahey National School in Kilmeena. She was born in June 1905 in Druminabo, Kilmeena, County Mayo, Ireland and was the daughter of John O'Boyle and Bridget McNally. Joseph and Catherine married on June 30, 1928 and they had eight children.

Joseph Redmond joined the Irish Army as a mechanic and was stationed in Athlone, a town on the Shannon River, County Meath. After he finished in the Army, Joseph was a driver for a Bakery Co. When WWII broke out there was no work in Ireland so he traveled to England for work, from 1940-1965. His family stayed in Ireland and he sent home all his wages. When Joseph retired, he retired home to Kilmeena, County Mayo, Ireland. Joseph Redmond died on July 18,1985 in Castlebar, County Mayo. His wife Catherine O'Boyle Redmond died on Feb 26,2005 in Castlebar, Co Mayo.

DONATED 3/1/2016 BY GRANDSON AIDEN REDMOND,
    WORKS OF ALLERGAN
BORN IN LIVERPOOL ENGLAND, LIVES IN WESTPORT, COUNTY MAYO,
    IRELAND

Bernard Feeney

born 1809
Ballyness, Antrim, County Derry, Northern Ireland

BERNARD FEENEY MET AND MARRIED Elizabeth McElvar in 1834. Elizabeth McElvar was also born in County Derry in 1811. They had seven children. In 1846 the family immigrated into America to Philadelphia, Pennsylvania. On the, voyage over to America, a Measles Epidemic broke out and two of their seven children died aboard the ship, from the Measles.

When they landed in Philadelphia, the family, continued, on to Wilmington, Delaware to be with other Feeney relatives that were already living in Wilmington. In 1860 the Feeney's lived at 525 East 5th St and at this address Bernard is listed as a laborer.

Bernard Feeney died June 21, 1871 at the age of 61 years old. He was buried in "The Old Catholic Cemetery" at 12th and Madison Streets, Wilmington Delaware. His wife Elizabeth McElvar Feeney died July 17,1878.

DONATED ON 4/9/2016 BY GR GR GREAT GRANDDAUGHTER
    DIANE ECKLES
BORN IN WILMINGTON, DELAWARE, LIVES IN NORTH WILMINGTON
NURSE MANAGER, MARRIED, 1 SON, 1 DAUGHTER, 5 GRANDCHILDREN

Dorinda Florence (Dot) Moriarty

born 1885
County Galway, Ireland
Parents: James Bowen Moriarty 1848-1930,
Margaret Emily Topham 1857-1934

IN 1912 DORINDA MORIARTY MET Arthur Ortestes Grey in Dublin Ireland. Arthur was born in 1884 in Hong Kong China. They married in 1912 and had one son. Dorinda Moriarty Grey died March 19, 1959 in Belfast Ireland at the Royal Victoria Hospital. Her husband Arthur Grey died in 1980 in Belfast, Ireland.

DONATED 3/14/2016 BY MARY JANE KIRBY
BORN MELBOURNE, VICTORIA AUSTRALIA, LIVES IN COCKATOO, MELBOURNE
WORKED AS A RECEPTIONIST FOR A DOCTOR'S OFFICE
MARRIED, 2 SONS, RETIRED

John Darcy

born 1828
County Clare, Ireland
Parents: John Darcy, Ellen McGuane

JOHN DARCY IMMIGRATED INTO AMERICA in 1850. He could not read or write. In 1853 he was living in Montreal, Quebec Canada. John met and married Mary Moran, who was from County Kildare, Ireland. They were married in Notre Dame Basilica in Montreal, Canada on April 25,1853. John and Mary first moved to Boston, Massachusetts, then in 1859 they moved to Refugio Texas, which was an Irish settlement were 200 Irish had immigrated to in 1834. John and Mary eventually had ten children.

Here in Refugio Texas, John purchased a wagon and horse and started hauling freight and people. On April 1865, it was the last meeting of War Court. They approved reimbursement of 61 bushels of corn. Which in turn John gave to families of the Confederate soldiers. Because he delivered this food and supplies to families of the Confederate soldiers, John was charged with helping the Confederacy. One condition of his parole was that he take the Oath of Amnesty and swear Allegiance to the U.S.A. No record was found of John becoming a citizen, only his Oath of Intent 1865 and 1867.

At the age of 42 years in 1870, John owned his own home and ranch. He next bought the Old Mission Hotel in Refugio on Alamo Street. John was now a Hotel owner, Farmer, Rancher and a Teamster with wagons and horses.

The U.S. Census of 1892 has the family name listed as Corcy. On Dec 19, 1893, on her birthday, John's wife Mary died. On May 31, 1901 John Darcy's Mission Hotel, was one of the 1st of 12 subscribers of the new Telephone Service in Refugio, Texas.

John Darcy died Feb 24,1901 of Tuberculosis at the home of his daughter Margaret in Beeville Texas, at the age of 76 years. He was buried at Mount Calvary Cemetery in Refugio, Texas.

DONATED ON 4/4/2016 BY GREAT GRANDSON JOSEPH DORCE
BORN IN HOUSTON TEXAS, LIVES IN MERCEDES TEXAS
RETIRED FROM AT&T

Annie Molly

born 1884
Falls Road, Belfast, Northern Ireland
Parents: William Henry Molly 1858-1886,
Roseann Britton 1858-1935

WILLIAM HENRY MOLLY WAS FROM Gifford, County Down, Northern Ireland. Roseann Britton was from Belfast, Northern Ireland. William Molly worked in a mill as a hackler, preparing the Flax before it was spun. In this linen mill, he met his wife Roseann Britton. Roseann was a weaver in the same mill. They married and had two girls, Mary, and Annie.

William Henry had decided to take the family to live in Kilburnie, Ayrshire Scotland. On the boat, over to Scotland, Henry got sick, mostly likely Tuberculosis (TB) and he never recovered. By 1886 the family was back in Belfast and William Henry had died, leaving his wife Roseann, a widow with two small girls. Roseann was unable to work and look after the girls so they were sent to the nuns, in Whitefield (outside the city) where they received a very good education.

In 1893 Roseann remarried to James McManus and the girls returned home to Belfast. Roseann has three more children with James McManus, Francis, Clara and Nelly. Roseann is very busy taking care of the young children.

As the Mary and Annie get older they planned to leave home. Annie trained as a seamstress. Mary marries Joseph Kerr and moves into her own home. Annie wanted to see the world and first travel to England to visit her Grandmother. She needed to raise the money for her passages and got a job as a servant for a rich family. While working for this family Annie meets a young, rich Canadian named George Perkins, who is related to her employer.

George Perkins was born in Petrolia, Ontario Canada. Petrolia Ontario was one of the first places in North America where oil was discovered. George's Grandparents were the original farmers who found oil on their land. His family had a lot of experience in drilling for oil. As the oil, had run out in Petrolia, George's family was recruited to help drill in other parts of the world. As, a result of this, George had not been brought up in Canada, but in Galicia (an area that straddles Poland and the Ukraine). Where his father and Uncle had owned successful oil and drilling companies.

George was fluent in German, French, Polish and Ukrainian. Annie and George fell in love and married with the disapproval of bother families. Annie's family because she was marring a man not Catholic, and George's family because he was marrying an "uneducated Irish girl". Annie moved to Galicia to be with George, where he and his cousin Karl where running the Polish end of the family oil business. While his brother and father ran a branch in England.

Annie's life was very different from her old life in Ireland. Galicia was described by the Austrians as the end of the World. She now had to learn Polish language, customs and traditions. Overnight she had a house full of servants and the possibility to purchase anything she wished from Paris, London, Vienna or St. Petersburg. George gave her a car and she learned to drive. They always traveled 1st class. Annie socialized with German and Polish nobility, went to endless parties and balls.

Now is the outbreak of WWI and no one in the family can get in touch with Annie. On the outbreak of the War everything has changed for Annie in Galicia. Suddenly, She, (was Irish) and George (was a Canadian) who bought had British passports were enemy aliens. It was particularly hard for George where he grew up in Glaicia and considered it home. Annie and Georges home were right in the middle of the Eastern front, directly in the path of the invading Russian Army. Not only did they not have the right papers to flee, but the military had requisitioned all trains so there was no easy way of escape. They went up into the hills to hide. The Russian Army had broken thru. As the, fighting had subsided they decided to go back to their home.

The surrounding countryside had been destroyed, crops ruined, there was almost no food and homes had been looted. The Russians were now in charge, they were no longer enemy aliens.

In 1915, the tide turned and Russia is retreating. They decide to head for Russia, not wanting to be caught as enemy aliens again. They get caught up in the second battle of Lemberg and find the station and railways being bombed. They took the first train which took them to Kiev.

In Kiev, for the first time in George's life the live on a budget. They have no access to their money in bank accounts. Here they lived in a Flat and stay put and worried that their money would run out. In 1917, everything changed with the overthrow of the Czar. George and others in the apartment block would stand guard with weapons to make sure their homes were not raided.

They decide they will try to travel the length of Russia on the Trans-Siberian Railway to get to the Pacific to go to Canada. They get as far as Moscow, where fighting is heavy and foreigners are not welcome. Civil War is all around them.

They get to Vladivostok and they can see in the distance Japan. Here George was able to get a job as a journalist, writing and English language column. It was not until 1919, they were, able to get a boat across the Pacific and Annie finally gets her wish to see Canada on their trip back to Ireland.

After the War Annie and George return to Strji. Everything has changed. There Oil Company is forced to take a Polish partner. After Georges Father and brother die they sell and move to Kensington, an exclusive area of London England.

Now it is March 1939 and WWII is coming. George got a job in London at Reuters News Agency. He is worried about Annie with all the bombing. So, During this time in WWII, Annie goes to live with her sister Mary and their cousin in Saltcoats, Scotland. So, she is safe and escapes the bombing taking place in london, England. After the War, Annie goes back to her husband in London. Annie Molly Perkins died in 1953 in Kensington, London England and was buried in Brompton Cemetery. After Annie died George was very sad, he went to Worthington England, which was by the sea, where his sister Florence lived. George Perkins died in 1955 in Worthington England.

DONATED 5/12/2016 BY GR GREAT NIECE CLAIRE MELVIN
BORN IN INVERNESS SCOTLAND, LIVES IN SOUTH LONDON
PUBLISHER FOR A MIDDLE EAST LAW FIRM, MARRIED, 2 CHILDREN

Catharine Feeney

born 1836
Ballynesse, Antrin, County Derry, Northern Ireland

CATHARINE FEENEY IMMIGRATED INTO AMERICA in Jan 28, 1848 with her parents when she was 12 years old. They arrived on the ship S.S. Scotia in Baltimore, Maryland. They settled in Wilmington Delaware. Later Catharine lived at the home of the John Willis Family as a servant.

In Delaware, Catharine met and married George W. Turner. George Turner was born in 1832 and was a Protestant and Catharine was a Catholic. At the time of their marriage, Catharine was 21 years old and George was 25 years old. They had six children. George was a Tailor for J.T. Mullins and Sons Clothing Store on 6th Street and Market St. in Wilmington, Delaware. George Turner died in 1884 and was buried at the old Ashbury M.E. Church.

After George's death, Catharine moved to 603 Market Street and ran a boarding house to support herself. On Jan 31, 1901 Catharine Feeney Turner died and was buried at Lawn Croft Cemetery, Delaware County, Pennsylvania.

DONATED 4/9/2016 BY GR GR GR GRANDDAUGHTER DIANE ECKLES BORN IN WILMINGTON DELAWARE, NOW LIVES IN NORTH WILMINGTON NURSE MANAGER, MARRIED, 1 SON, 1 GIRL, 5 GRANDCHILD

James Mullin

born 1/18/1818
County Londonderry, Northern Ireland
Parents: Henry Mullin, Ann Diamond
They were Farmers

JAMES MULLIN WAS BORN IN Derry, officially Londonderry, which is the second largest city on Northern Ireland.

In May 12, 1845 at the age of 27 years old, James Mullin left Ireland and immigrated to America aboard the ship, S.S. Fannie. James traveled with his brother Cornelius and his sister Grace. They landed in Philadelphia Pennsylvania and moved on to Dubuque, Dubuque, Iowa where James settled and made his home.

James met and married Mary A. Kingsley in 1876. Mary A Kingsley was born Feb 28, 1855 and was a native from Plymouth, Massachusetts. They had nine children. He was a Catholic and a Democrat. In Dubuque James purchased 200 acres of farm land. As a Farmer, he was a hard worker and retired to enjoy his declining years. James Mullin died on Feb 20,1896 and his wife Mary Kingsley Mullin died on Jan 4,1934.

DONATED 4/22/2016 BY GR GRANDDAUGHTER PAM MULLIN
BORN AND LIVES IN DUBUQUE IOWA. RETIRED,
   WORKED IN SOCIAL SERVICE AND TRAINED EMPLOYEES TO SELL MAJOR APPLIANCES, FOR A LARGE APPLIANCE MANUFACTURER.

James Kelaher

born 4/21/1847
Mohill Parish, Country Leitrim, Ireland
Parents: William Kelaher, Ann Wren

JAMES KELAHER EMIGRATED FROM IRELAND to America in 1873 and arrived in the Port of Boston, Massachusetts, then traveled north and decided to settle in Salem, Massachusetts. The family surname in Ireland was Keligher and when James settled in America the spelling of the name was changed to Kelaher.

James met and married Ellen McGoven. Ellen was the daughter of Patrick McGovern and Mary Farley, of County Meath, Ireland. They had three children and rented a home at 62 Bridge St, Salem, Massachusetts. James worked in a factory as a leather worker. In 1940 the family moved to 70 Washington St, Salem, Mass.

James, had a heart problem, that caused him to pass out and appear to be dead. On at least two occasion this did happen and Ellen started to prepare a Turkey and other foods for the wake and then he revived and was fine.

When he actually, pass away, Ellen did not have the money to buy the extra food for his wake. James Kelaher died on April 21,1847 in Salem, Mass. After his burial Ellen McGovern Kelaher went to live with her daughter Eleanor and grandchildren in Hyde Park, Mass, where she stayed till she died on Dec 6, 1943.

Donated 4/2/2016 by Great Granddaughter Kathy McKinnon
One of 10 children, born in Quincy, Mass
Office Administrator in medical offices and
   Medical Insurance Environments.
married, 1 son, 1 Daughter, 1 grandson.

Patrick Joseph Conway

born 10/15/1884
Loughloon (Lagloon), Westport, County Mayo, Ireland
Parents: Patrick Conway 1831-1902,
Ann Mulryan 1841-1925

PATRICK JOSEPH CONWAY WAS THE youngest of eight children. He immigrated into American on Sept 24, 1906 on the ship S.S. Carmina arriving at Ellis Island, New York. He was supposed to go to Brookline, Massachusetts and live with his brother Michael and family but instead went to Canadaigua, New York to stay a while with his older brother John and Family. From New York, Patrick traveled up to Canada and did mining jobs. He had listed his residence as Edmunton, Alberta Canada, living with his cousin Patrick O'Connor. At the age of 30 years, Patrick came down thru the border crossing at North Dakota. In 1910 Patrick put a claim in at the bureau of land grants and got 199 acres of land two miles south of Medora, North Dakota. A lot of the land could not be cultivated. Patrick had horses, cows, chickens, cats, and dogs.

Thru a pen pal club Patrick meets and marries Pauline Marie Kaelberer. Pauline was born 1894 and was from Medora North Dakota. On April 1919, they elope. Sometime before Patrick got married he broke his right ankle. The doctor only came into town every three months and his ankle got infected. He ended up having three amputations above the knee and had to have a wooden leg. Patrick and Pauline had five children. Patrick worked as a janitor-custodian at the Court House and the school house. He didn't have much of a formal education but he loved to read. Patrick did register for the WWI Draft. Patrick Conway also had a lot of stomach problems and was diagnosed with Lung Cancer and died on Nov 8, 1942. After he died the land was sold and his wife remarried.

(Story was obtained from letters from Patrick's daughter, Patricia Conway written to Clare Conway)

DONATED ON 4/1/2016 BY GREAT GRANDNIECE CLARE CONWAY BORN IN NORTH QUINCY MASS, RETIRED IN SPRING HILL FLA

Thomas O'Brien

born 9/25/1845
St. Peter's Church Drogheda, County Louth, Ireland
Parents: James 1821-1879, Bridget Russell 1822

THOMAS O'BRIEN WAS BORN IN County Louth, Ireland. In Irish, the county is called Lù. It is the smallest of Irish counties, hence its nickname: The Wee County.

During the Potato famine, the O'Brien Family moved to Benefieldside, Durham, England. On May 22,1871 Thomas O'Brien immigrated to America on the ship S.S. Wyoming and arrived in New York City, New York. From New York, Thomas continued, on to south west Pennsylvania to the borough of Derry, where he found work in the Steel Mills. Thomas's job was as an Iron Peddler.

In 1871 Thomas met and married Martha Matilda Nickels in Pittsburgh, Pennsylvania. Martha Nickels was born Mar 6,1857 in Wilmore, Cambria, Pennsylvania and was the daughter of August Nickels and Catherine Collins. Martha had raised 12 children and was a housewife. On Oct 2,1891 Thomas became a Naturalized Citizen in Connellsville, Fayette, Pennsylvania. Thomas O'Brien died in 1916 of Influenza. Martha Nickels O'Brien died on Sept 8,1941 of Arteriosclerosis in Aliquippa, Beaver, Pennsylvania.

DONATED 4/19/2016 BY GREAT GRANDDAUGHTER
AUDREY O'BRIEN NELSON
BORN IN ALIQUIPPA, PENNSYLVANIA. LIVES IN TAMPA FLORIDA,
MARRIED, 2 CHILDREN, RETIRED RESEARCH SCIENTIST.

Catherine McVeigh

born 1826
Ballycastle, County Antrim, Northern Ireland
Parents: James McVeigh, Mary McKay

CATHERINE MCVEIGH MARRIED THOMAS MEEHAN on Jan 1, 1848 in Ballycastle, County Antrim, Ireland. They had two sons Francis and Charles. Thomas passed away in 1851. Catherine remarried shortly thereafter. She married a man named Alexander McArthur. Alexander and Catherine had four children; Ellen, Mary, Alex and Patrick.

In 1863 they decided to immigrate to America. As their departure time came nearer, Ellen contracted a communicable disease and was not able to make the journey. She and her older brother Francis stayed home in Ireland with Catherine's sister, Elizabeth McVeigh Church. They had to wait a few months to get passage on a ship to America.

Catherine, Alexander and their four children boarded the ship S.S. Adelaide out of Liverpool England and arrived in New York City on April 6, 1863. They had a difficult time crossing the Atlantic Ocean. Many of the passengers became ill and several died. Their son Patrick died on board the ship and was buried at sea.

The family settled in New York City in a tenement house for three years where Catherine Ann and Daniel were born. Tragedy struck again when children Mary and Alex died in New York of food poisoning.

In 1866 the Family moved to rural Wayne County, northeast Pennsylvania, where Catherine had family. Here her husband Alexander took a job in a local tannery. In 1873 Alexander purchased property in

High Lake, Wayne County, that the family farmed the land for six years. While living in Pennsylvania two more children were born, another Mary and another Alex.

The older boys Francis and Charles Meehan left Pennsylvania and headed to Omaha, Nebraska where they found work in the Smelters. The rest of the family left Pennsylvania in 1879 to join Francis and Charles in Nebraska. Alexander and Catherine along with Francis and Charles were granted 160 acres each in the Leo Valley of Greeley County, Nebraska under the Homestead Act, that they farmed for many years.

Alexander McArthur died in 1889 and his wife Catherine McVeigh Meehan McArthur died in 1923 at the age of 97 years. They were buried together in Calvary Cemetery, Omaha, Nebraska.

Donated 9/27/2016 by Great Grandnephew George Church
Born in Brooklyn, New York, lives in South Town, Long Island New York
Married, retired 1 son, 3 grandsons

Mary Ann Linden

born 1825
County Kerry Ireland

MARY'S MOTHER DIED WHEN SHE was an infant. Her Father and the older children left to go to America and settled in Rochester New York. Mary was left in Ireland to be raised by her Aunt. In Kerry Ireland, Mary was friends with Thomas White and they planned to go to America together. Thomas White was born in 1825 in Kerry, Ireland.

Thomas left Ireland first in 1845 and arrived in Canada. From Canada, he traveled down to New York and then on to settle in Carbondale, Pennsylvania. Once he had established himself he sent for Mary.

Mary arrived in Castle Garden New York on July 7, 1846 on the ship S.S. Sir C Campbell. It was listed as a famine ship. Thomas White had gone to New York to meet Mary, but, her ship had been delayed, by a storm at sea. Upon not finding Mary, Thomas went back to Carbondale, Pennsylvania. When Mary's ship landed, there was no one to meet her. Mary could not read or write and had no money. She came across an Irish Policeman, who befriended her. The Policeman took Mary to his home and wrote to Thomas to come get her. Mary stayed at the home of the Officers family until Thomas arrived.

After Thomas arrived, Thomas and Mary went to visit Mary's Father and her family in Rochester, New York. Mary's family, the Linden's had become very Americanized over the years, and they were very ashamed of Mary's old country ways. Thomas and Mary left the house to have no further contact with the Linden family ever again.

Thomas and Mary married in 1846 and had eight children. In 1850 they lived in Rochester, Monroe, New York. By 1870 they lived in Carbondale, Luzerne, Pennsylvania. In 1885 the family had moved to Freeman Valley, Greeley, Nebraska. They homesteaded land in Nebraska and Thomas is a farmer. In 1885 Thomas is suffering from a disease of his eyes and becomes totally, blind. Thomas died Aug 13, 1899 and is buried in O'Connor, Greeley County, Nebraska. Mary Ann Linden White died on Nov 9, 1904 at the age of 79 years

DONATED 3/26/2016 BY GR GREAT GRANDDAUGHTER MARY COLEMAN
BORN AND LIVES IN EAU CLAIRE WISCONSIN
LPN, DIVORCED, 5 CHILDREN, 4 GRANDCHILDREN

Patrick Green

born 1846
Ballina, County Mayo Ireland
Parents: John Green 1820, Sabina Cosgrave 1820

PATRICK GREEN, WAS BORN IN the middle of the famine. In Ballina, which is a small town in north County Mayo, by the River Moy. His family toughed it out and he became a cattle dealer like his father. Patrick then married another child of the famine, Sabina Gillespie. Sabina Gillespie was from Knock, County Mayo, Ireland a neighboring town just 15 minutes from Ballina.

On March 22, 1876, Patrick, married Sabina Ann Gillespie in Kilmoremoy, Killalal, County Mayo Ireland. Patrick gave up the cattle business, although, it is not known why. They had thirteen children from 1877 to 1901 and raised eleven of them in Ballina on his meager salary as a "sanitary officer".

Patrick Green died Aug 13,1917 and was buried at the Leigue Cemetery in Ballina, County Mayo Ireland.

DONATED 3/1/2016 BY GREAT GRANDDAUGHTER
  AUDREY ELAINE CROSSMAN PECK
BORN IN MIDDLEBURY, VERMONT.
  LIVES IN PLAISTOW, NH
MARRIED, 2 SONS, 2 GRANDDAUGHTERS, RETIRED TEACHER

Annie Lennon

born 6/14/1864
Knappabeg, Aghagower, Westport, County Mayo Ireland

ANNIE LENNON IMMIGRATED TO AMERICA and arrived at Ellis Island New York in 1888. From New York she moved on to Philadelphia, Pennsylvania. In 1889 she met Thomas Gannon, who was the son of Michael Gannon and Bridget Heneghan. Thomas was born May 1864, in Owenwee, Westport, Co Mayo Ireland. He was a Moulder/Laborer and had already been living in America, at 537 Alaska St. in Philadelphia PA. for a few years.

Annie married Thomas Gannon on May 5,1889 in the Annunciation Blessed Virgin Mary Catholic Church, 1511 South 10th St. in Philadelphia, Pennsylvania. Witnesses were Augustus Grady and Maria Shields. In 1890 they lived at 1211 Chubb St, Mildred, Philadelphia, PA.

Thomas Gannon died on Oct 28,1940 of a cerebral hemorrhage at the age of 76 years. Annie Lennon Gannon died No 21,1943 in her 4, bed room Townhouse at 4283 viola St, Philadelphia PA. They were buried together at Holy Cross, Yeadon, Delaware County, Philadelphia.

DONATED 3/24/2016 BY GRANDNIECE AGGIE LENNON
LIVES IN PHILADELPHIA PA. RETIRED

Cornelius Lyhane

born 9/29/1867
Ballyvourney, County Cork, Ireland
Parents: Daniel Lyhane 1852,
Johanna Sweeney 1837-1865

COURNELIUS LYHANE WAS BORN IN the village of Ballyvourney, in southwest County Cork. Ballyvourney is an Irish word, meaning Town of the Beloved.

Cornelius Lyhane emigrated from Ireland to America and arrived at Ellis Island, New York City, New York on May 4,1879, aboard the ship S.S. Baltic of the White Star Line. Cornelius continued moving on and arrived at Little Rock at Higgenson, Arkansas. He immediately went to work on the Iron Mountain Railroad.

In 1881 Cornelius met Annie Foley, who was from Lexington, Fayette County, Kentucky. They married on Aug 15, 1881 and lived at Valley Hot Spring Garland, Arkansas. They had eight sons and three daughters. In 1908 Cornelius takes his wife Annie and son Daniel back to Ireland to visit his family. 1909 Cornelius moves his family to Moberly, Missouri and he takes a job as Road Master on the Railroad and is then made head boss of a railroad section.

Cornelius's wife, Annie Foley Lyhane died on May 29, 1947 in Bartlesville, Washington, County, Missouri. Cornelius Lyhane died in 1952 in Bartlesville, Oklahoma and was buried back in Missouri with his wife.

Donated 3/16/2016 by Gr Grandniece Maryagnes Lenahan Born in New York, Queens, lives in New Jersey, Married, 2 daughters, retired Hospital Pharmacist.

Margaret ("Maggie") Cunniffe

born 2/25/1885
Meetrane, Ballyhaunis, County Mayo Ireland
Parents: John Cunniffe 1849-1928,
Bridget Lyon 1848-1928

MAGGIE CUNNIFFE WAS THE 4TH of seven children. In 1904, at the age of 19 years old, she emigrated from Queensland Ireland aboard the ship S.S. Majestic and immigrated to New York City, New York. She eventually settled in Philadelphia Pennsylvania, where she worked as a maid and became a U.S. Citizen.

Six years after immigrating, she returned to Ireland and brought her younger sister, Annie back to the states with her. Annie also settled in Philadelphia, Pennsylvania and later married and raised a family.

In her 20's Maggie met Patrick (Paddy) Joseph Mullin at Atlantic City, New Jersey at a wet Tee shirt competition. Patrick Mullin was born on June 30, 1879 in Slieve, Dummore, County Galway Ireland. Maggie and Paddy married in 1914 In Philadelphia, Pennsylvania which is where they raised four children.

Maggie Cunniffe is remembered for her keen sense of humor, hard work, and her devotion to family and church. He life ended at the age of 63 years old at St Joseph Hospital in Philadelphia. She died from acute Intestinal Obstruction caused by Cancer of the Bowel.

Her husband Paddy was bereft. Descendants claim Paddy was lost without Maggie and didn't know how to do anything for himself. Maggie has spoiled him rotten. Maggie Cunniffe Mullen died on Feb

16,1949 and Paddy Mullen died Jan 6, 1963 in Chester, Delaware Co, Pennsylvania. Both are buried at Holy Cross Cemetery Yeardon, Delaware Co, Pennsylvania.

Donated 4/23/2016 by Gail Edna Vogel
Margaret (Maggie) Cunniffe is the grandmother of Gail's brother-in-law Patrick Allen Lawrence.
Lives in suburbs of Philadelphia PA, Retired

Martin Fadden

born 2/20/1885
Ballyglass, Westport, County Mayo Ireland
Parents: Michael Fadden 1867, Bridget Staunton 1866

MARTIN FADDEN WAS THE OLDEST son of seven children. He had five brothers and two sisters. He grew up in the small farming village of Ballyglass. Ballyglass is Gaelic and means (The Green village).

In 1912 Martin immigrated to America, arriving at Ellis Island, New York on May 5,1912. He continued, on to Chicago, Illinois to live near his cousins Thomas Berry and Mary Berry Scahill. Martin became a U.S. Naturalized Citizen and served in WW1. He was stationed in Macon, Georgia Aug 9, 1918.

Mary Agnes Joyce was born Feb 3,1888, the daughter of Mary Reddington and Michael Joyce in Roslahan Manulla, County Mayo Ireland, she was their youngest and only daughter. Mary Agnes traveled with her brother Thomas to America to visit their Uncle Dennis Joyce, who lived in Scranton, Pennsylvania in 1908. Thomas remained in America and Mary Agnes returned to Ireland. In Oct 1920 MaryAgnes immigrated to America, this time to Chicago, Illinois to live with her Aunt Mary. In this time, her brother Thomas and her Uncle Dennis Joyce relocate to Chicago, Illinois, and they are all together. Martin met Mary Agnes Foley and they married on April 6, 1921, in Chicago. Mary Agnes is 33 years old. Martin finds work with the Chicago Transit Authority. They had four boys during their marriage.

Mary Agnes Joyce Fadden died in 1962 and the oldest son died in 1964. After these deaths that Martin had, he goes with his youngest son to El Monte, California. Martin Fadden died on Sept 24, 1965 at the age of 80 years and was buried in Evergreen Park, Illinois.

Donated 3/25/2016 by Grandson Austin Fadden
Born in Chicago Illinois, lives in Knoxville Tennessee
Married, Retired, 2 boys, 2 girls

Anne Brennan

born 5/13/1877
Newmarket on the Fergus, County Clare Ireland
Parents: James Brennan 1851-1928,
Katherine (Kate) Malley 1852-1910

ANNA BRENNAN WAS ONE OF ten children. She immigrated to America in 1898 arriving at Ellis Island, New York, New York. She went to visit her sister Mary and then, returned to Ireland. In 1904 Anna and her sister Helen went to America to New York City, New York to visit their brother John.

In 1910 Anna took a brief trip back home to Ireland when her Mother died, then she went back to New York. Anna partitioned for Naturalization on Jan 11,1954, #720050, Alien Registration: 7818372 New York, New York.

Anna met and married Michael Madden on June 24, 1924. Michael Madden was born on Sept 28,1880 in County Galway, Ireland. Anna and Michael lived at 1157 Second Ave, Manhattan, New York. Anna was the proprietress of a candy store, which was on Second Ave. Anna's husband Michael Madden passed away at the Bellevue Hospital in Manhattan, NY. Anna Brennan Madden died Sept 30,1965 and was buried at Gates of Heaven Cemetery, Valhallee, New York.

DONATED 3/15 2016 BY GREAT NIECE MARYAGNES LANAHAN BORN IN NEW YORK CITY, NEW YORK. LIVES IN NEW JERSEY. MARRIED, 2 DAUGHTERS, RETIRED HOSPITAL PHARMACIST.

Thomas Clancy

born 2/15/1825
County Galway Ireland
Parents: John Clancy, Ellen Costello

THOMAS CLANCY IMMIGRATED TO AMERICA in 1846 at the age of 21 years on the ship S.S. David. He first settled in Maryland and when he did get settled, Thomas sent for his brother and his Mother. In 1827 Thomas moved to Geneva Illinois and he worked as a night agent in the depot for the C & N West Railroad. At this time there were only seven boarding houses and residence, in the vicinity, of the depot, which were only wooden shanties with a wood burning stove for heat. His first job included climbing the tussle at night when the trains departed the Depot to put out the sparks that the train left behind in the station. Thomas Clancy worked for the Railroad for 45 years with no pension.

In June 1850 Thomas met Elizabeth Allen, who was born in 1827. They married in St. Charles, Illinois at Turner Junction on April 4, 1853. Thomas and Elizabeth had 5 children in 18 years. In 1855 Thomas purchased a lot of land in Geneva Illinois to grow potatoes.

In 1866 Thomas and his brother Patrick, who was a stone cutter, built a lime stone home. The home that they built is still standing today. The Geneva Illinois Historical Society awarded the Clancy family home an Historical Landmark with a Plaque. Thomas Clancy died on Dec 12, 1902 at the age of 77 years

Donated 4/14/2016 by Gr Gr Granddaughter Mary Leipold
Born in Chicago, Illinois, lives in Bensenville Illinois
President of Ladies Ancient Order of Hibernians.

Dennis Conway

born 1835
Ballina, Westport, County Mayo Ireland
Parents: Michael Conway b-1798 Co Mayo Ireland
d-1866 Gloucester, Quebec Canada; Bridget Doherty
b-1811 Easky, Co Sligo, Ireland, d-1881 Gloucester,
Quebec, Canada

DENNIS CONWAY WAS 4 OR 5 years old, in 1840 when he emigrated with his parents and sisters Anna and Margaret and brother John to Quebec Canada. They settled and farmed a plot of land in Lower Canada. Today it is known as Chelsea, Quebec, Canada. The Conway's were a founding family in Gloucester which is now a part of Ottawa, Canada. They were a respected Catholic Family. Dennis was a farmer and he also worked in a rock quarry.

In 1851 the Conway Family moved to Russell County where they farmed. Russell County Township is located south-east of Canada's Capital of Ontario. Later Dennis started a business picking up milk from local Dairy Farmers and delivering the milk to the Dairies for processing.

Adjacent to their farm was a farm belonging to Amble Louis Cyr, his wife Marie Esther Aubuchon Cyr, and their five children. Here Dennis meets Jane Louise (Eugenia) Cyr, one of M.r Cyr's daughters. Jane Cyr was born 1839 in Ottawa. They married on June 1864 in Gloucester, Ontario Canada and have 7 children. In 1866 Dennis's Father died from respiratory complications. Later in life, Dennis suffered with severe Dementia and he died in 1903. His wife Eugenia died 1912 in Ottawa, Canada.

Donated 5/2/2016 by Gr Great Grandson Ron Conway

Born Ottawa, Canada Lives in Donaldson Lake, Buckingham, Quebec

Married, retired design builder, General Contractor

James Joseph Costello

born 7/17/1860
Upper Pallas, Borrisoleigh, County Tipperary Ireland
Parents: James Joseph Costello Sr 1811-1901,
Johanna Maher 1836-1906

JAMES COSTELLO WAS ONE OF eight children that grew up on a farm, to be a farmer in Tipperary. He met Sarah Ryan and they married in 1890. Sarah Ryan was born Dec 17, 1865, the daughter of Dennis Ryan and Ann Carr. They lived in the next town over, in Coolderry, Borrisoliegh. In Ireland, they had three children, two sons and one daughter.

James realized that there was no work for him Ireland and went to the Christian Brothers for help. They were, able to obtain a job for James in as a farmer and a Boiler Operator at the Troy Male Orphanage Asylum in Troy, New York, USA.

In 1897 James and his wife, two daughters and one son left Ireland and arrived in New York City, New York. They continued, on to the eastern coast on the Hudson River to the city of Troy, Rensselaer, New York. When they arrived at the Orphanage, they are given a house next door to the Orphanage to live in.

In 1898 their son Daniel is born in Troy, New York and they live at 126 Bedford St, in Troy, New York. James eventually stopped working at the Orphanage and started collecting garbage on a horse drawn cart and he is a teamster, working for the Troy Public Works Department and he has two more children.

In this time, the oldest son is forced to drop out of school to go to work to help the family. Also, Mary, the 12 year, old daughter is forced to go to work. She worked in a collar shop.

James Costello died Jan 17, 1948 and his wife Sarah Ryan Costello died on Feb 4, 1946 and are buried together in Troy, New York.

Donated 6/27/2016 by Great Grandson Matthew Costello Born in Rochester, New York, Single, Disabled, worked as a Restaurant Manager and worked at Kodak making film

Maurice Histon

born 5/20/1848
County Limerick, Ireland

MAURICE HISTON WAS BORN IN County Limerick, in the Mid-West region of Ireland. Maurice Histon immigrated to Australia in 1863 and settled in Sydney where he had a job as Victualler, Landlord of the Albion Hotel. It was here Maurice met an Irish Housekeeper named Catherine Hudson. They married on April 1875. At this time, Maurice became insolvent and the family moved to Armidale, New South Wales. They had 8 children.

Maurice worked as a Line Repairman for the Armedale Post Office until 7/1896. His wife Catherine Hudson Histon died on Nov 1896. After Catherine died, Maurice moved back to Sydney with seven of his children. Maurice Histon died in 1917 and was buried with two of his sons.

DONATED 4/22/2016 BY GR GR GREAT GRANDDAUGHTER ROSE LEE
LIVES IN GUNDALAR, QUEENSLAND, AUSTRALIA
ARTIST, GRAPHIC DESIGNER, BOOKKEEPER

Mary McQueeny

born 1832
Drumshanbo, County leitrim, Ireland
Parents: John McQueeny, Mary Kelly

THE MCQUEENYS WERE A VERY poor family that lived in the small town of Drumshanbo. They ended up with their children going to and residing in the Workhouse in Drumshanbo. This was a very hard time in Ireland with the potato famine and a young family to feed and no money. John and Mary McQueeny decided to send their older daughters, overseas and give them new lives.

Daughters, Bridget age 18 years and Mary age 17 years were sent to Australia as part of the Earl Grey Program. They went to England and boarded the ship S.S. Lady Peel out of Plymouth on March 14,1849. The girls arrived in Sydney, Australia on July 6,1849 as Famine Orphans. Neither Bridget or Mary could read or write. From Sydney, they made their way to Brisbane, where Bridget found work as a housemaid.

Mary met James Cash, who was born in Birmingham England in 1804. James is 29 years her senior, is 5' 3" tall with brown hair. He was a convict, convicted for Armed Robbery of leather from Thomas Whitehouse in England and sentenced to death but given a reprieve to seven years and transported to Australia aboard the ship S.S. Florentine in 1830. His trade and occupation was Pressure Hinge Dresser and fitter. James received his letter of freedom on Jan 24,1842.

On Oct 27,1849 Mary and James married at St. Stephen's Church in Brisbane. They were married by Fr. James Hanley, the first resident Priest in Brisbane. They then move to Darling Downs area and settle on the southern bank of the Southern Pine River.

James erects a slab home made from the Red Cedar on their land. The walls have holes bored into them for rifles to be placed during Aborigine attacks. There were a few attacks on the home and the last one was in 1860 when Mary was hit in the back with a Nulla Nulla (an Aborigine war club) while James was away with the cattle. She was forced to flee her home and hide in the bush till the attackers left.

James and Mary were very hospitable people and would always have a tin of tea on the stove for visitors. Mary was an exceptional Horsewoman and used to ride in shows. James spent a lot of time away from the home and Mary was left to raise the children by herself.

On Sept 9 1860, while James and Mary were out milking the cows, their, daughter Ellen's night close caught fire and she received severe burns and died from her injuries.

Mary was notified of the death of her Father in Ireland. After the death of Mary's Father, John McQueeny, her husband James sponsored for Mary's Mother and sisters Catherine, Elizabeth, and Alice along with her brother John to come to Australia.

Mary's husband James Cash died on Dec 13, 1870, two years later Mary remarried Edward Cain. Mary McQueeny Cash Cain died on June 29,1913 and was buried with her husband, Edward Cain at Albany Creek Cemetery in Brisbane, Australia.

DONATED 2/27/2017 BY GR GREAT GRANDNIECE JENNIFER ROOKS
BORN IN DALBY, QUEENSLAND, AUSTRALIA
MARRIED, 3 SONS, 3 GRANDCHILDREN, RETIRED FROM EDUCATION

Michael Hamilton Lennon

born 1/12/1895
Fair Green, Westport, County Mayo Ireland
Parents: Stephen Lennon 1856, Sarah J Green 1858-1900

MICHAEL (GUSSIE) LENNON LIVED IN Westport, County Mayo Ireland his whole life. He was a member of the Westport "A" coy of the 3rd Battalion of the Old IRA. In 1911 Gussie lived at High St in Westport. He was very happily married to his wife Mary and they had 2 sons and 1 daughter. Gussie was a Tailor and in 1970 he moved his family to Claremorris, County Mayo, a neighboring town from Westport and here he had a very successful Tailoring business at the back of McGarry's Drapery Shop. His wife wife Mary Lennon died Sept 7, 1963 in Claremorris. Gussie retired from his shop in 1970.

Michael (Gussie) Lennon died on Aug 17,1973 in Claremorris, Westport, County Mayo and was buried at Banacarroll Cemetery, Claremorris, Westport, County Mayo.

DONATED 3/24/2016 BY NIECE AGGIE LENNON
LIVES IN PHILADELPHIA PENNSYLVANIA, RETIRED

Michael (Gow) Sullivan

born 1845
Clonee, Kenmare, County Kerry Ireland

Michael (Gow) Sullivan was a Farmer, Horseman and Blacksmith in County Kerry. His nickname, Gow, means Blacksmith.

Michael married Julia Doyle in 1866. Julia Doyle was born Aug 15,1847 in Derreendaragh, Kenmare, County Kerry. They lived on Ormond Island in Kenmare and were tenants of the Marquis of Lanscowne. They had eight children all born in Kenmare in Tuosist Parish and Clonee Parish.

In Feb 16,1896, the Sullivan Family departed from Ireland and immigrated to America, arriving and landing in New York City, New York. In New York, they met up with the older children who had already moved to America and were living in Nassau, County, New York. Michael and Julia lived in different areas of Nassau County with their children. The census shows that Michael never worked while he lived in New York.

On Feb 6,1916 Michael Sullivan died in Hempstead, Naussau, New York and was buried at St. Mary Star of the Sea Cemetery in Lawrence, Nassua Co, New York. His wife Julia Doyle Sullivan died on March 24,1931 in Hewlett, Nassau, New York and was buried with her husband.

Donated 5/4/2016 by Gr Grandson Michael Richard Sullivan Born in Astoria, Queens New York, Lives in Hamden Connecticut
Social Worker, single

Our Lady of Knock Queen of Ireland

On August 21, 1879 at 8pm, 15 people from the village of Knock, Co Mayo Ireland witnessed an apparition of Our Lady, St. Joseph, St. John the Evangelist. Witnesses watched in the pouring rain, reciting the rosary for 2 hrs. Our Lady was described as deep in prayer with her eyes toward Heaven. Alto it was very dark, witnesses could still see the figures very clearly. Archdeacon Cavanagh was the Parish Priest at Knock at the time of Our lady's visitation. He is buried in the Knock Parish Church. Knock Parish Church is now a Shrine in Ireland. Most of the people of Southern Ireland are Roman Catholic and highly cherish this event. There are statues and grottos to Our Lady of Knock all thru Ireland.

We Pray for all the Wonderful souls mentioned in this book.

Hail Mary, full of grace.
Our Lord is with thee.
Blessed art thou among women,
and blessed is the fruit of thy womb,
Jesus.
Holy Mary, Mother of God,
pray for us sinners,
now and at the hour of our death.

Novena To Our Lady Of Knock

IN THE NAME OF THE Father, and of the Son, and of the Holy Spirit, Amen. Give praise to the Father Almighty, To His Son, Jesus Christ the Lord, To the Spirit who lives in our hearts, Both now and forever. Amen.

Our Lady of Knock, Queen of Ireland, you gave hope to your people in a time of distress, and comforted them in sorrow. You have inspired countless pilgrims to pray with confidence to your divine Son, remembering His promise. Ask and you shall receive, seek and you shall find.

Help me to remember that we are all pilgrims on the road to heaven. Fill me with love and concern for my brothers and sisters in Christ especially those who live with me. Comfort me when I am sick, lonely or depressed. Teach me how to take part ever more reverently in the Holy Mass.

Give me a greater love of Jesus in the Blessed Sacrament. Pray for me now, and at the hour of my death. Amen.

Mary Agnes O'Leary

born 9/29/1880
Ballingeary, County Cork Ireland
Parents: Cornelius O'leary 1853-1904,
Margaret Lyhane 1860-1882

IN COUNTY CORK, IRELAND, MARY Agnes O'Leary had taken the exam to be a teacher but instead she left for America and did not teach. Mary Agnes O'leary immigrated to America May4, 1899 thru Ellis Island, New York, New York. She resided at 160 E48th St, New York. In 1905 Mary Agnes met Michael Francis Brennan. Michael was from County Clare, Ireland. They were married at St. John the Evangelist Catholic Church, on 55th St and 1st Ave, New York. They had two daughters.

In 1909 Mary Agnes took one daughter back to Ireland for the family to see. On returning home to New York she brought her sister Katherine, who wanted to emigrate to America. In 1918 she had become a Naturalized Citizen thru her husband. In 1932 she returned to Ireland with her husband Michael and two daughters to visit her family.

Her husband Michael Brennan died Jan 26,1971 in Woodside, New York at the age of 90years old. They had been married for 65 yrs. Mary Agnes O'Leary Brennan died Jan 29,1980 at the age of 99 yrs.

DONATED ON 3/16/2016 BY GRANDDAUGHTER MARYAGNES LENAHAN BORN IN QUEENS, NEW YORK, LIVES IN NEW JERSEY
MARRIED, 2 DAUGHTERS, RETIRED HOSPITAL PHARMACIST

Annie Whelan

born 7/9/1882
Tintern, County Wexford, Ireland
Parents: Daniel Whelan, Ann Hanlon
Married 1872 Ballycullane, Tintern, County Wexford,
Ireland

ANNIE WHELAN WAS THE 5TH of seven children of Daniel and Ann Whelan. They lived in the small town of Tintern, on the hook Peninsula of County Wexford.

Ann met and married Daniel Keating in New Ross, County Wexford Ireland in 1917 and they had five children. Daniel owned and ran a General Goods Shop in the Main St of New Ross. The family lived above the shop. They were a family well off, for they had help in the home for chores such as ironing. During the War and the Depression, Daniel gave credit to people who were struggling, which resulted in the loss of his business.

Annie Whelan died March 27, 1960 at the age of 85 years old. She was buried in St. Bridgid's Churchyard, Terrerath, New Ross, County Wexford Ireland.

DONATED 3/9/2016 BY GRANDSON HUGH O'REILLY
BORN IN NEW ROSS, CO WEXFORD, IRELAND, RETIRED, MARRIED 4
  CHILDREN
STUDIED TO BE A CHEMICAL ENGINEER AND WORKED IN THE OIL
  INDUSTRY.

Ann Murphy

born 1833
County Meath, Ireland

IT IS BELIEVED, BY THE family that Ann Murphy was one of the first female orphans to come to Australia in 1850 aboard the Ship John Knox. The John Knox was one of the Ships that carried young female Irish orphans 14-20 years old from Irish Workhouses. On arrival, the orphans were taken to Hyde Park Barracks and into employment, mostly as house servants.

In 1852 Ann married an English convict Joseph Aldington at St. Michael's Church of England, in Wollongong on Aug 31,1852. Joseph signed his name and Ann made her mark. They had a daughter Sarah Ann. Joseph was convicted at Gloucester Quater Session in March 1847 for stealing fowl. He was sentenced to 7 years and sent to Australia.

In 1854 Joseph's, sentence had expired and the Family was no longer restricted to staying in Wollongong. They moved to St. George, Sydney and Joseph changed his name to Holdington. In 1854 they had a son, Joseph Jr. In 1858 Joseph was in trouble and appeared in Central Police Court. He was committed to Darlinghurst Gaol, he was warrented as insane on April 16,1858 and sent to Tarban Creek Assylum. Joseph's madness was thought to be hereditary as he had an Uncle insane and his daughter Sarah Ann was later committed as being of unsound mind. While Joseph was in Tarban Creek, his pregnant wife Ann was unable to care for he two children. Ann was forced to have them admitted to the Randwick Asylum for Destitute Children on May 1858. Sarah was

5 years and Joseph Jr was 3 years old. On Aug 20,1858 Ann had her 3rd child Catherine. In Oct 1850 Joseph was considered cured discharged and he went home. They went to get their children back but were only given Joseph Jr. Sarah was found of unsound mind and was sent to Parramattie Mental Hospital where she stayed till she died at the age of 14 years old in 1867.

On June 13, 1859 Joseph is again readmitted to Tarbn Creek and dies at the Asylum on June 30,1859 and he was buried there. On June 1861 Ann remarried to Bernard Hammell at St. Mary's Catholic Church in Sydney Australia. They both sign with an X. They have 5 children. In Nov 1872 Bernard was killed in a freak accident. His Dray (a strong cart with no sides) capsized.

In July 1887 Ann Murphy Hammell died at her home at Iredale St, Newtown Sydney. She was buried in an unmarked grave in the Catholic Section of Rookwood Cemetery

DONATED 4/15/2016 BY GREAT GRANDDAUGHTER ROSE LEE
LIVES IN GUNDALAR, QUEENSLAND AUSTRALIA
ARTIST, GRAPHIC DESIGNER, BOOKKEEPER, RETIRED, 3 CHILDREN, 4 GRANDCHILDREN

Mary Hopkins

born 5/30/1872
Larganboy, County Mayo Ireland
Parents: David Hopkins b- 1838, Larganboy, Co Mayo,
Ellen Murray b- 1846, Bekan, Co Mayo Ireland

Mary Hopkins met John Finnegan, who lived in the next town of Bohogue, County Mayo. John Finnegan was born in 1866, in Bohogue, Ballyhaunis, County Mayo, which is just down the road from the Knock Shrine.

They married and had ten children and one that died. Mary's husband John Finnegan died in 1918 and Mary was left to raise the children on her own. Mary Hopkins Finnegan died Aug 26, 1938 in Bohogue, Ballyhaunis, County Mayo. Mary had 9 children and 49 Grandchildren.

Donated 4/3/2016 by Granddaughter Cecilia Turner
Born in San Francisco California, she is a twin
Lives in Millbrae California, 4 children, 5 grandchildren

Peter Ambrose Lennon

born 6/8/1890
Fair Green, Westport, County Mayo Ireland
Parents: Stephen Lennon 1856,
Sarah J Greene 1858-1900

IN 1901 PETER LENNON, WHO was a Blacksmith was living at Carrowmalurgan, Westport, County Mayo.

On April 18, 1907 Peter departed from Queenstown Ireland and immigrated to America where he arrived at Ellis Island, New York City, New York. He went to live with his sister, Sarah, who lived at 604 Dudley St., Philadelphia, Pennsylvania. It was Sarah that paid his passage to come to America.

In 1913 Peter met Mary Hannigan and they married on May 21, 1913 at the Epiphany of Our Lord, Catholic Church in Philadelphia, PA. They had eleven children.

In 1917 Peter registered for the Draft for WWI. Also in 1942 he registered for the draft for WWII. On the 1910 and 1920 census Peter is listed as a Horse shoer for a Blacksmith Shop at South Jessup St. Philadelphia, PA. In 1940 Peter is listed as a Bartender for a Saloon. Peter died Jan 1977 at Cape Mary, Cape Mary County, New Jersey, at the age of 87 years old.

DONATED 3/24/2016 BY DAUGHTER AGGIE LENNON
LIVES IN PHILADELPHIA PA.

Daniel Gallagher

born 5/29/1879
Ardara, County Donegal Ireland
Parents: Patrick Gallagher 1833-1927,
Margaret Boyle 1852-1934

DANIEL GALLAGHER LEFT HOME AT the age of 15 years old to travel to Northern Ireland, where he worked in a shipyard. He then traveled to Scotland and London, England to find work. When he had saved enough money, he boarded a ship to Canada.

Daniel traveled thru Canada, and entered America, at the border crossing at Montana. In Montana, Daniel worked on Ranches and in the Mines. Then he moved on to New York. It was in Prospect Park in Brooklyn New York where Daniel met Annie McGinley. Annie was born April 1, 1886 and was from Faugher, Glencolmcille, a coastal village in south-west Donegal Ireland. Daniel and Annie married in New York City in 1910. They had three children.

Annie yearns to go back home to Ireland. Annie and her three children, Ann, Marion and Joe go back to Ireland in 1916. They went to Ardara, to the home of Daniel's parents. Daniel followed his wife to Ireland in 1920 when he has saved enough money to buy a farm. Ann has purchased land in Fintra, Killybegs and from here they can see the Atlantic Ocean.

Daniel and Annie have three more children and now Daniel is tired of farming and wants to go back to New York. They agree and Daniel returns home to New York in 1926. Several months later he falls off the back of a truck and factures his skull, dying a few days later. Annie comes back to America to claim his death benefits but she has, to leave the three youngest children in Ireland because the immigration quota, is, filled at, this time. She returns to Ireland in 1928 to bring her children back to New York to be reunited with their siblings.

In New York, Annie buys a large 2 family home where she takes in boarders. At this time, her 3 oldest children go to work to help pay the mortgage and pay bills. Annie McGinley Gallagher died on Oct 31, 1958 in Brooklyn New York. She is buried with her husband at Holy Cross Cemetery, Brooklyn New York.

DONATED 3/8/2016 BY GR GRANDDAUGHTER MAUREEN DYER ICKRATH BORN IN BROOKLYN NEW YORK, LIVES IN BETHANY BEACH, DELAWARE WORKED IN MARKETING FOR GEORGE'S COMMUNITY COLLEGE MARRIED, 1 SON, 1 DAUGHTER, 2 GRANDSONS, RETIRED

Lawrence (Larry) Newell

born 5/1847
Ardrumkilla, Killower Parish Belclare, County Galway
Ireland
Parents: James Newell 1802-1887, Bridget Byrne

LARRY NEWELL WAS ONLY A baby when his mother Bridget Byrne died in County Galway. His father had remarried to Catherine Lally 1824-1911 and they had six more children, Patrick, John, Honora, Bridget, Sarah, and Matthew. Larry was employed at Castlehackett "The Big House" as a caretaker for the landlords, the Kirwan family.

It was in church Larry met Margaret Greaney. Larry said: He fell in love with her when she walked down the church aisle with her golden braids hanging down her back. Margaret Greaney was born 1856 to Patrick Greaney and Mary Monahan, of Ballentleva, Ardrumkilla, Beclare, Tuam, Co Galway Ireland.

They " romantically eloped", when Margaret's parents were in town making final arrangements for her to marry another man. Larry and Margaret later married in Oct 1880 in the Belclare Catholic Church. They had a daughter Bridget "Delia" in July 1881.

In May 1882, they immigrated to America, to Portland Maine, were there was a very large Irish community and where they already had relatives residing there.

Larry was a very tall, rugged, strong man. He and Margàret spoke Gaelic among themselves and with friends from the old country but never taught their children. In Maine Larry worked on the Androscoggin

Railroad as a brakeman from middle 1880's until his retirement. Then he worked as a janitor at the railroad offices until his final retirement in 1925 at the age of 79 years. The year he retired, Larry and Margaret moved from the old Irish neighborhood in St. Dominic's Parrish, in Portland to a new house they had built the way they wanted to live in. Margaret was a saver, she paid $10,000 cash for their new house.

Larry Newell died Sept 28, 1940 at the age of 94yrs, at his home on 106 Bedford St. Portland Maine and was buried in Calvary Cemetery in South Portland Maine.

DONATED 6/10/2016 BY GR GREAT GRANDSON
   MATTHEW JUDE BARKER
BORN AND LIVES IN PORTLAND MAINE
WRITER, GENEALOGIST, AND HISTORIAN AT THE MAINE IRISH
   HERITAGE CENTER
PORTLAND MAINE.

Martin Michael Morrison

born 9/15/1886
Foxboro, County Mayo Ireland
Parents: Michael Morrison, Mary Clark

MARTIN MORRISON IMMIGRATED TO AMERICA on April 1909, where he landed in New York City, New York and moved on to Pittsburgh Pennsylvania. In Pittsburgh, he met Mary Jane Hoban. Mary Jane was born Sept 1, 1890 in Westport, County Mayo Ireland and she emigrated to America in May 1909. They married on Aug 7, 1912 at St. Brendan's Catholic Church, Pittsburgh Pennsylvania and had six children.

Martin worked in the Steel Mills until they closed in 1929. He then moved his family to Chicago Illinois where he found work in a Steel Mill. Martin Morrison died June 9, 1930 in Chicago Illinois of Pneumonia. His wife Mary Jane Hoban Morrison died Feb 14, 1956 of Pneumonia.

DONATED 3/10/2016 BY GRANDDAUGHTER MAUREEN GOINS
BORN IN CHICAGO, ILLINOIS, RESIDES IN NEW LENOX, ILLINOIS
MARRIED, 3 CHILDREN, 7 GRANDCHILDREN
MY GRANDFATHER WORK HARD AND DIED YOUNG. I WISH I KNOW MORE ABOUT HIM.

Michael Conway

born 8/1/1871
Loughloon, Westport, County Mayo Ireland
Parents: Patrick Conway 1831-1902,
Ann (Nancy) Mulryan 1841-1925

MICHAEL CONWAY WAS ONE OF eight children, four brothers and three sisters of Patrick and Ann Conway. He attended the Brackloon National School in Loughloon, Westport, County Mayo Ireland. Michael immigrated to America in 1891 arriving on the ship S.S. Eturia in the Port of Ellis Island, New York on Nov, 19, 1891. He had several cousins and two brothers, already living in New York and Massachusetts. He was sponsored by and his Uncle McFadden to come to America. Michael continued, on to Brookline Massachusetts where he worked as a laborer, digging ditches and working on making new roads for the Parks Department of Town of Brookline Mass. Later he became a Teamster.

He married Mary Stanton on Sept 26, 1900 whom he knew from back in Westport, Ireland, at St Mary's Catholic Church, Brookline, Massachusetts. Mary Stanton was born in Jan 6, 1880 in Carrowholly, Westport, County Mayo, Ireland, and immigrated to America after Michael to the Port of Ellis Island, New York, on May 23, 1897. Here she continued, on to Boston, Mass to meet with Michael. They lived with relatives at Pearl St in Brookline then moved to 18 Aspinwall Ave, in Brookline, Mass. Michael and Mary had eleven children, seven that lived.

Michael was said to be a very tall and quiet man. He didn't smoke but he did drink. For breakfast, he ate what was called, Bull's Milk.

oatmeal with whiskey in it. 1904 he applied to become a Naturalized Citizen and received his U.S. Citizenship on July 25, 1923. Michael was a member of the Catholic Order of Forresters and was buried by the Catholic Church. He died on Sept 11, 1954 and was buried in the family Plot at St. Joseph's Cemetery in Jamaica Plain, Massachusetts.

Donated 2/23/2016 by Granddaughter Clare Conway
Born in North Quincy, Massachusetts, single,
  retired in Spring Hill, Fla
Worked in Boston, Mass. at Mass Eye & Ear Infirmary

Catherine (Kate) Connell

born 8/15/1889
Cuiltybo, Claremorris, County Mayo Ireland
Baptised 8/25/1889
Parents: Michael Connell 1851-1911,
Margaret Lavin 1824-1904

KATE CONNELL EMIGRATED FROM QUEENSTOWN Ireland to America with her sister Mary Agnes on the ship S.S. Teutonic, arriving at Ellis Island, New York on March 19, 1907. Kate was engaged to marry a man in New York City, New York, However, he died.

They, continued, to Malvern in Chester County. Pennsylvania. When Kate and Mary arrived in Malvern Pennsylvania there was no official Catholic Church. So Mass was held at a residence in area called Riley Banks. They held card parties and social here. At this residence, Kate won a beauty contest.

From 1910-1920, she was a servant for the Warner Estate in Malvern, today, it is the Villa Maria Academy. Working here Kate meets John Newhaus, who was a delivery man for his parent's bakery. On May 10, 1922, they marry at St Patrick Church. Kate becomes a full- time wife and Mother, never to return to Ireland.

John found work with the railroad. Catherine (Kate) Connell Newhaus died in a nursing home in West Chester Pennsylvania on Jan 16, 1966. Her husband John Newhaus died in 1960 and they were buried in St Ann's Catholic Cemetery on Pothouse Road in Phoenixville PA.

DONATED 4/25/2016 BY MARY ROBINSON
BORN IN MALVERN, PENNSYLVANIA, LIVES IN MILTON, DELAWARE
RETIRED U.S. GOVERNMENT, MARRIED, 1 SON, 2 GRANDSONS

Anna Frances Maguire

born 6/14/1894
Killmallock, County Limerick Ireland
Parents: John Maguire, Bridget Eileen McDonald

ANNA MAGUIRE LEFT IRELAND FROM Queenstown on the ship S.S. Saxonia. and immigrated to America and landed in Boston Massachusetts on Aug 11, 1910 when she was 16 years old. Her brother John and her Mother's sister, Ann McDonald, sponsored Anna's trip to America. Anna's brother John stays in Ireland and lived in Ballymac, Charlesville, County Limerick Ireland.

From Boston, Massachusetts, Anna continued to travel north until she arrived at Cross St, Lowell, Massachusetts, where her Aunt Anne lived. Later her sister Eileen arrived, but she moved on to Oxford Mass to live. It was here in Lowell that Anne met her childhood sweetheart, Walter Henry Smith. Walter Smith was born Feb 17, 1893 in Lowell Mass. Walter Smith worked as a Machinist in a Machine Factory. Anna found work as a Velvet Packer in a Cotton Mill. Walter and Anna married in Lowell, Mass. on Nov 1917. In 1920 they moved to Crawford St and rented and They then had a daughter Margaret. Also in 1920, Anna became an American Citizen.

In 1930 they moved and rent at 15 West Ninth St. in Lowell. They now have three children, Margaret 11, Claire 7 and Claudia 4. In 1933 their only son Walter (Sonny) was born. Anna and Walter had 22 grandchildren. Anna McGuire Smith died May 29, 1972. Walter Smith died on June 6, 1973. Granddaughter Sandra remembers her Grandmother Anna having a thick Irish accent. Sandra said her Grandmother was cheerful and sweet. Sandra also remembers the Orange Pineapple juice her Grandmother would give her. Sandra remembers her Grandfather, Grampy, sitting out on the porch smoking his cigar. He would always smile at her. She asked, "Why are you smiling"? Her Grampy would reply: " You, because I love you"!

Donated 5/6/2016 by Granddaughter Sandra Lee Smith Houle
Born in Lowell, Massachusetts,
　lives in Manchester, NH
Married, 2 children, Retired RN

Martin Logan

born 1884
Glinsk, County Roscommon Ireland
Parents: Thomas Lohan, Mary Mannion

MARTIN LOGAN IMMIGRATED TO AMERICA in 1900, arriving at Ellis Island New York. Passing thru Ellis Island, his name got changed from Lohan to Logan. Martin started his life as a stock boy for the Great A&P Tea Company in Long Island, New York City, New York. He met and married Lillian Amos, who was only 16 year old at the time and they had three children. Working at the Supermarket, Martin was forced to retire at the age of 65 years old and at that time he was store manager, on Main Street in Flushing, New York.

It was said Martin was a man that would kneel at your bed to say your evening prayers. He was a quiet man 5' 5" tall and weighed 140 lbs. Martin Logan died in 1957. His wife Lillian Amos Logan was 93 years old when she died in Levittown, New York.

DONATED 4/9/2016 BY GRANDSON JOSEPH LOGAN
BORN NEW YORK CITY, WORKED IN THE U.S. ARMY, RETIRED.
MARRIED, 1 SON, 3 DAUGHTERS, 7 GRANDCHILDREN.

Maurice Hugh O'Connor

born 2/11/1821
Clash, Kilquane, County Kerry, Ireland

MAURICE O'CONNOR MET AND MARRIED Catherine Martin on 2/22/1846. Catherine Martin was born 11/8/1818 in Garrane, Kilmalkedar, (Corkaquiney Barony), County Kerry Ireland. Catherine was one of 7 children of James Martin and Catherine Moriarty. They married on Feb 22, 1846 in Bally Ferriter, County Kerry, Ireland.

In 1847 Maurice and his wife emigrated from Ireland to America arriving first in Canada. They made their way down to Massachusetts where Maurice found work laying railroad tracks. He laid tracks in Massachusetts and then up thru Vermont. In 1849 the Railroad era arrived in Brattleboro, the southeast corner of Vermont, with the opening of the Vermont and Mass. line, to the cities of Southern Connecticut Valley. At, this time, Maurice settled in Brattleboro and continued working as a Brakeman for the Railroad.

Maurice O'Connor died on Oct 12, 1898 in Vermon St. Reeds Hill, Brattleboro Vermont. His wife Catherine Martin O'Connor died on Dec 10, 1886 in Brattleboro, Windham, Vermont. They are both buried at St. Michael's Catholic Cemetery. His Obituary said he was one of the first Irishmen to settle in Brattleboro, Vermont.

DONATED ON 4/15/2016 BY GR GREAT GRANDDAUGHTER
   MARY O'CONNOR TOSSEL
BORN IN HARTFORD, CONNECTICUT MARRIED, RETIRED RN.

Robert Burrows

born 1826
Westport, County Mayo Ireland

ROBERT BURROWS LEFT IRELAND AND immigrated to America and landed in June 1, 1844 in the Port of Boston, Massachusetts. From Boston, he continued, on to Portland, Maine, where there was a very large Irish population. In Portland, Robert went looking for work, he was a Boiler Maker by trade.

In Portland, Robert met Mary Ann Quinn Shields. Mary was born in Portland, Maine on Oct 6, 1826, the daughter Philip Quinn and Mary Ann Weeks. Her Father Philip was from Goland, Stranolar, County Donegal Ireland. Mary, whom had been married before, her husband Edward Shields died in 1847. Robert and Mary married on Oct 27, 1849 and had eight children in 16 years, all the children were born in Portland, Maine. But only three lived to be adults, William Henry, Francis Day, and David Bacon. Roberts oldest son William became a Boiler Maker with his Father. They all lived in Cumberland, Portland Maine.

In 1872 the family travelled across the United States by train to settle in San Francisco, California. Robert and his sons got jobs working on the Central Pacific Railroad. Robert became the Assistant Foreman of the Railroad Companies Boiler Shop.

At the age of 50 years Robert got pneumonia and died on Jan 19, 1876 in Sacramento, California and was buried in Colma, California. Flags in all the Railroad Shops were lowered to half-mast out of respect for his memory.

Donated 6/8/2016 by Great Granddaughter Valerie H Burrows
Born Oakland California, Lives in Sacramento California
Works as a Facility Administrator and Theater Manager

Ellen O'Sullivan

born 3/19/1859
Russagh, Skibbereen, Glan Cork, County Cork, Ireland
Parents: Daniel Sullivan b-1832, Mary Goggins b-1831

ELLEN O'SULLIVAN WAS THE YOUNGEST of four children of Daniel and Mary Sullivan. The Sullivan's owned their own farm land in Skibbereen. Skibbereen is a Town in County Cork, on the southern tip of Ireland. The name Skibbereen is Irish and means little boat harbor.

This was during the Great Potato Famine of the 1840's. The Skibbereen area in County Cork was one of the worst areas effected, by the famine. Skibbereen was a thriving market town, trading in linen, wool and agricultural products. It was devastated by the Great Famine of the 1840s. Not a loaf of bread or a pound of meat to be found anywhere. Many people who couldn't read or write and had no money preferred to live by the old barter system, trading goods and labor for whatever they needed. If they had money, they couldn't find a single loaf of bread to purchase. The grains were shipped to England. The Irish in the countryside began to live off wild blackberries, ate old cabbage leaves, edible seaweed, shellfish, roots, roadside weeds, and even green grass. They sold the livestock to pay the landlords. People starved and died by the roadside.

Daniel and Mary with their four children: Timothy b-1855, Mary b-1856, Hanora b-1858, and Ellen b-1859, sold their farm and moved and purchased land near Schull and here they had five more children:

Catherine b-1862, Florence b-1864, Margaret b-1867, Annie b-1870, and Daniel b-1874.

Daniel died in 1893 and his wife Mary died 1903. Both were buried together in St. Mary's Cemetery in Schull. Their daughter Mary took over the farm.

Now to escape the effects of the famine the children started to leave Ireland and Immigrate to other countries to find work and make a new life. Timothy went to America. Daughters Ellen and Hanoria left and immigrated to Australia, to the colony of Queensland.

1880 Hanoria joined the Sisters of Mercy at all Hallows in Brisbane, taking the Name of Sr. Philomena and was transferred to the convent in Rockhampton, Colony of Queensland where she received her religious habit in 1882. 1899 she died from Pleurisy and Rheumatoid Arthritis. She was buried in the religious section at Bowen Cemetery in North Queensland, Australia.

Ellen travelled to Roma in West Queensland in 1881 to work as a housemaid at "Hope Creek" the home of Bridget McQueeny Bowden. Here Ellen met Thomas Bowden, the Bowden's eldest son. Three of Ellen's youngest sisters now came joined her in Roma from Ireland. Ellen and Thomas married in 1882 and they had eleven children, five boys and six girls. Ellen's husband Thomas Bowden died on Dec 6,1923 of a stroke and Ellen O'Sullivan Bowden died on Nov 27, 1934. They were buried in the McQueeney-Bowden family plot in the Roma Cemetery, Queensland, Australia.

DONATED 2/27/2017 BY GREAT GRANDDAUGHTER JENNIFER ROOKS
BORN DALBY, QUEENSLAND, AUSTRALIA
MARRIED, 3 CHILDREN, 3 GRANDCHILDREN
RETIRED FROM EDUCATION

Patrick Bannon

born 1806
Foilduff, County Tipperary Ireland

PATRICK BANNON WAS FROM TIPPERARY, a famous area for the horse breeding industry. Patrick met Bridget Blake was born in 1801 and was from Knockfune, County Tipperary, Ireland.

He married Bridget Blake on June 27,1825 in Newport, Tipperary. The church records have them listed as Paddy and Biddy. Since this was only 10 miles from where they lived, they traveled to the church on a Pony cart. Bridget must of been pregnant when they wed as their first child, John, was born in Sept of the same year. They settled in Foilduff, County Tipperary. Son John must, of died for there is no record of him but they did have a son Michael, who was born in 1827 in Foilduff.

In 1830 Patrick and his family emigrated from Ireland and moved Quebec, Canada. They first settled, in Argenteuile on the east side of the Ottawa River near Carillon. In 1835 they received a land grant across the river in Sainte-Marthe Vandreiul, Quebec Canada. It was on a high ridge rather rocky land but potatoes grew well there.

Patrick and Bridget raised six children, Sarah, Bridget, Mary, James, John, and one son Patrick Bannon Jr born in 1840. Both Patrick Bannon and his wife Bridget Blake Bannon died in 1846, just 15 days apart from each other. Both in their early 40's. All the children were raised by different neighbors. Patrick and Bridget were buried in Sainte-Marthe Vandreiul, Quebec Canada.

Donated on 4/1/2016 by Gr Great Granddaughter MaryAnn Bannon Robertson

Born in Burlington, Ontario Canada, lives in Cambridge, Ontario Canada

Married. She is an Awarding Winning Teddy Bear Artist.

Isaac Langford

born 1790
Rosenallis, Ballyfin, County Laois Ireland
Parents: Joseph Langford, Martha Parkinson

THE LANGFORDS WERE FARMERS THAT lived between the small towns Mountrath and Ballyfin, on the Glebe Farm, which is in the south of the midland region of County Laois.

Isaac Langford met and married Maria Langford, they married in 1812 and had ten children. Maria Langford was born in 1793, the daughter of Isaac Langford and Maria (Betsy) Westman, in a small town in the North of County Laois called Mountmellick, on the Owenass River.

Maria's brother Thomas Langford had already emigrated to Ontario Canada so in 1832, Isaac, his wife Maria and their children ranging from 19 years old to a baby less than 1 year old boarded a ship out of Dublin Ireland for Canada. When they reached Canada, their intent was to meet up with Maria's brother Thomas, and settle in London Ontario area.

The three month, voyage to Canada was very tragic for the family as Cholera broke out on the ship. Both the parents Isaac and Maria died of Cholera as well as their 4 year, old daughter Jane and their baby died of the disease. Leaving the eldest son, 19 year old, Joseph to care for his siblings. On June 23,1832 the ship arrived at Grosse Island in the St. Lawrence River. From here they traveled to Hamilton, Ontario where they were to meet their Uncle Thomas. Upon landing, in all the confusion of the landing, all their chests with their belongings became lost. The eldest son Joseph was robbed of the family savings of gold coins which, was to be their financial security. Their Uncle Thomas arrived and met them and boarded all the children in a cart pulled by an Ox and took them to his home in London, Ontario.

All, of the children, with very little education worked very hard on the farm to make their live better. One of the children was Thomas, Joseph's brother. He was born July 6, 1822 in Mountvellick, County Laois Ireland and when he grew up and married Catherine Lannin and had his own family, he moved to Baysville in Northern Ontario. In the early 1870's Thomas moved to Baysville in Northerine Ontario where the land was cheap. Thomas Langford died Feb 1, 1895 and was buried at Basville Cemetery, Baysville, Ontario Canada.

DONATED 6/3/2016 BY GREAT GRANDDAUGHTER
 CHERYL LYNN PRETSELL
BORN IN TORONTO CANADA, LIVES IN GARIANOQUE, ONTARIO CANADA
3 CHILDREN, 1 DAUGHTER, 2 SONS, 3 GRANDCHILDREN, DIVORCED

Patrick Gallagher

born 1853
Fauleens, Carracastle, County Mayo Ireland
Parents: John Gallagher 1852-4/28/1891,
Margaret Flemming 1853
Married 5/11/1850

PATRICK GALLAGHER KNEW AND DATED Mary Foley in Carracastle, County Mayo. The family story, I, was told by a cousin in Ireland was that Patrick had been going out with Mary Foley whilst in Ireland. Mary Foley was born in 1856 in Baroe, Carracastle. They lived just 1 mile apart from each other. But Mary decided that she didn't want to see Patrick anymore and she left Ireland and went to America to live with her sisters in Boston, Massachusetts. Patrick was heartbroken and couldn't live without her. In 1880 Patrick followed Mary to America to Boston Massachusetts and convinced her to marry him.

They married in the Cathedral of Holy Cross in Boston, Massachusetts on Sept 6, 1877. After marrying, Patrick and Mary returned to Carracastle in Ireland where their first daughter Margaret was born in 1879. By 1881 Patrick and Mary had moved and were living in the Wigan area of Lancashire, England. Wigan and Charlestown have a history together and many families moved from Charlestown to work in the iron works and coal mines of Wigan, Lancashire England. Here Patrick found work as a Brickyard laborer before working at the Kirkles Iron and Steel Works, where he worked for the rest of his life. They seem to move quite frequently, as did most poor families at the time, they lived in 1901, at 3 Smith Street off

Belle Green Lane, Wigan, 1911, at 46 Bolton Street, Wigan, and in 1914, they lived at 49 Scholefield Lane, Wiggan, Lancashire, England. There was a very large Irish community around the Iron works with a corresponding large number of pubs. Unfortunately, most of the old houses in this area, have now been demolished.

Patrick and Mary had 8 children, Margaret b-1879 Charlestown, Mayo Ireland, John Patrick b-1881 Hindley, Lancashire England, Thomas b-1883 Wiggan, Catherine b-1886 Wiggan, Bridget b-1888 Wiggan, Mary b-1890 Wiggan, Patrick b-1893 Wiggan, and Annie b-1895 Wiggan, England.

Another family story I was told about Mary Foley and Patrick, was about when they were living in Wigan, perhaps in Bolton Street which would place this event, 1911. Mary apparently kept pigs. They were always moving and when living in Bolton St. something happened with Mary's pigs which resulted in the offence going to court where she would have been fined. Patrick went to court on her behalf, with a sum of money Mary had given him to pay the fine. When the judge announced the amount the fine would be Patrick smiled because it was less than the amount Mary had given him. The judge was unhappy about this and then fined Patrick for contempt of court.

Patrick Gallager died March 19, 1921 at 9 Scholefield Lane, Wigan. In his probate record the Patrick leaves £177 10s and his estate, is administered by his son Patrick.

DONATED 3/8/2016 GR GREAT GRANDSON MICHAEL GALLAGHER BORN AND LIVES IN HITCHEN, HERTFORDSHIRE ENGLAND. MARRIED, 3 CHILDREN, WORKED IN IT.

Ann (Nancy) Mulryan

born 1838
House 6, Laghloon, Knappa, County Mayo, Ireland
Parents: William Mulryan 1803-1883,
Honora Gill 1813-1885

NANCY MULRYAN LIVED AT THE residence at house 6 in Laghloon, Knappa, Westport, County Mayo, Ireland, and was baptised in St. Brendan's Roman Catholic Church Myna, Kilmeena, Westport, County Mayo about 1835.

The name Mulryan or O'Mulroyan is pre 10th century Old Gaelic O'Maoilriain. The name translated as " The Descendant of the worshipper of the Water God" Rian. Possibly her family was once Pagan.

Nancy married Patrick Conway and they had eight children. She and her husband were devote Catholics and she raised all her children in the Catholic Church. Patrick was born in 1831, a farmer, the son of Philip Conway 1790-1860 and Mary Tunney 1793 of Laghloon, Westport. They were tenants of the Marquis of Sligo.

Nancy was beloved by all her family. Years later the Grandsons still spoke lovingly about her, into their 60's. Her Portrait hung in the living room of her grandson Michael Conway's home in Brookline, Massachusetts.

Ann (Nancy) Mulryan Conway died on June 6, 1925 at the age of 81 years old and Is buried in the Aughogower Cemetary, Aughogower, Westport, County Mayo, Ireland.

Clare Ann Conway

Donated 4/20/2016 by Great Granddaughter Clare Conway
Born in North Quincy, Massachusetts,
 lives in Spring Hill, Fla
Worked at the Mass General Hospital,
Retired, single

Catherine Burns

born 1834
Leckanvy, Parish of Ovghaval, County Mayo, Ireland

IN 1856 CATHERINE BURNS MARRIED Michael Duffy, who she knew from her childhood, in Leckanvy, Coounty Mayo. They later immigrated to America and settled in Trenton, the Capital of New Jersey. Trenton, was established by the Quakers in 1679.

Sometime in America, Catherine's last name got changed from Byrns to Burns. Catherine and Michael had nine children, five that lived to adulthood. Catherine was a very fashionable dressed woman and was a very strong and independent person. Michael was a laborer that did odd jobs.

Catherine's husband, Michael Duffy, died in 1917 in Trenton, Mercer County, New Jersey, and was buried from St. Joseph's Church, in an unmarked grave at the Princeton Cemetery.

Catherine Burns Duffy died in March 5, 1928 in Croyden, Bucks County, Pennsylvania and was buried at St. Mary's Cemetery, in Trenton, Mercer County, New Jersey. There is no marker on her grave.

DONATED ON 3/1/2016 BY GREAT GRANDSON GEORGE DUFFY
BORN IN CORTLAND, NEW YORK, LIVED IN OREGON,
RETIRED, FORMER METAL HEALTH COUNSELOR

Michael J Callaghan

born 1864
Leamyglissane, County Kerry Ireland
Parents: John Callaghan, Margaret Healy,
Married in Rathmore, County Kerry 1856

MICHAEL CALLAGHAN EMIGRATED FROM IRELAND to America in 1882 on the ship S.S. Atlas at the age of 18 years old to the port of Boston, Massachusetts. Michael traveled north from Boston and settled in Malden, Massachusetts where he built his own home at 27 Whitman St., Malden, Mass. He was a laborer for the City of Malden.

Michael met Johanna Long and they were married at the Immaculate Conception Catholic Church on 5/17/1891 and they had 9 children. Johanna Long was born Feb 17, 1870 in County Cork, Ireland. She immigrated to America on the ship S.S. Cephalonia. Michael Callaghan received his Naturalization papers on Oct 27, 1886.

Michael Callaghan died in 1919 and his wife Johanna Long Callaghan died March 28, 1956. They were both buried at St. Mary's Cemetery in Malden Mass.

DONATED ON 4/10/2016 BY GREAT GRANDSON JERRY CALLAGHAN BORN IN MALDEN MASS, RETIRED U.S. ARMY AIR FORCE FLIGHT TEST CENTER, SUPERVISORY GENERAL ENGINEER.

James Patrick Lawlor

born 3/13/1868
Derreen, Ballysakeery, County Mayo Ireland
Parents: Henry Lawlor 1845-1925,
Bridget McHale 1845-1921

JAMES PATRICK LAWLOR WAS THE eldest of twelven children. In 1893, James had gone Out one day into the field to count cattle and never returns home. One year later the family receives a letter from James stating that he is in America.

James immigrated to America on the Ship S.S. Germanic on July 13, 1894 at the age of 24 years. He arrived and settled in New York City, New York. Here he married his childhood sweet heart, Margaret McHale, who was from a nearby town of Kincon in County Mayo, Ireland. They married on June 9, 1895 in St. Catherine's of Genoa, Roman Catholic Church in New York City, New York. Margaret, over the years, gives birth to eleven children, of whom only three lived to adulthood; James Joseph Lawlor, Richard Francis Lawlor, and Gerald J. Lawlor.

James takes work as a hotel doorman then goes into hotel security. Eventually working at the Waldorf Astoria Hotel in New York City. On Sept 26,1920, his wife Margaret McHale died in New York City, New York and is buried Calvary Cemetery in Woodside, Queens, New York.

In 1923 in New York City, New York James remarries for a second time, to Agnes Elizabeth Toomey. Agnes was born Nov 24, 1884 in Wilmington Delaware. They had a daughter Miriam Frances Lawlor Curio.

James Patrick Lawlor died on June 4, 1945 in Bronx, Bronx Co, New York and is Buried with his 1st wife Margaret in Calvary Cemetery, New York. His wife Agnes Elizabeth Toomey Lawlor dies in 1958 in Toledo Ohio and is buried at Calvary Cemetery.

Donated on 4/21/2016 by Great Grandson
 Michael Richard Sullivan
Born in Astoria, Queens, New York, lives in Hamden
 Connecticut.

Joseph McClare

born 1798
Castlederg, County Tyrone, Northern Ireland
Parents: John McClare, Ann Bell

IN 1816, AT THE AGE of 18 years old, Joseph McClare left Londonderry, Ireland on aboard a ship for Halifax, Nova Scotia, Canada. On his voyage, Joseph made two friends, Anthony Wellwood and Thomas Hopkins. The ship landed in Halifax, Nova Scotia and the three young men continued, on to Rawdon, in the county of Hants, Nova Scotia where they found employment with Mr. Hugh Barron.

Mr. Barron owned a Saw and Grist Mill and Joseph and his friends went to work at the Mill. Joseph worked at mills most of his working life but, like everyone at the time, he was also a farmer.

Joseph met and married Isabel Barron and they had eight children. Isabel Barron was born about 1800 in Rawdon, Nova Scotia, Canada. She was the eldest of the thirteen children, of Hugh Barron and Lydia S. Potter. Joseph bought a farm in South Rawdon and built his own home of hewn timber walls, shingled roof, and a stone chimney. Joseph and Isabel live in this home until his wife, Isabel died in 1863. Isabel Barron Mc Clare was buried in St. Paul's Churchyard in Center Rawdon, Nova Scotia, Canada.

Joseph Mc Clare died in the spring of 1884, at the home of his son Andrew and family in Brooklyn, Hants, Nova Scotia, Canada, and he was buried beside his wife.

Donated 7/15/2016 by Gr Great Granddaughter
 Gail Ellen Laskey
Born in Windsor, Nova Scotia Canada, lives in Wolfville, Nova
 Scotia, Canada
Married, 3 children.

Dominick McGrail

born 1/26/1893
Derrygarrow, Louisburgh, County Mayo Ireland
Parents: John Mc Grail, Mary Egan

DOMINICK MCGRAIL WAS BORN IN a small town of Louisburgh on the southwest corner of Clew Bay in County Mayo. The town of Louisburgh was constructed by John Denis Browne, the 1st Marquess of Sligo.

Dominick McGrail left Ireland on the ship S.S. Cymric and immigrated to America and landed in Boston, Massachusetts. On arriving in Boston, Dominick changed the spelling of his surname from McGreal to McGrail. As many of his cousins had done that had come to the United States ahead of him. From Boston, Dominick continued, on out west to Worcester, Massachusetts. He settled in Worcester where he worked on Street Cars and later served on the Worcester Police Department for 36 years.

Dominick was a self, taught musician. He played 4 instruments and was a talented Step Dancer. It was said he had very strong hands. Dominick once used his hands to put out the flames on a young neighbor's boy who caught on fire while jumping over a pile of burning leaves. This earned him a citation from the Worcester Police Department. He received numerous commendation by the Police Department. He also served in WWI, with the U.S. Army seeing action in the Western front of France.

Here in Worcester, Dominick met Mary Ann Heraty, who was born July 7, 1903 in Derrymore, Drummin, Westport, County Mayo Ireland.

She came to America on the Ship S.S. Celtic. Mary Heraty was one of eleven children of Thomas Heraty and Mary O'Malley.

Mary and Dominick met at a Kitchen Racket in Worcester, Massachusetts. A Racket is a party celebration party. They married in 1928 in Worcester, Mass. and they had five children, Mary, Dominick, Maeve, Sean, and Grainnie, and were married for 51 years. Mary understood the importance of sending her children to college. As an education was something no one could take away from you. She recited verses and poems that she loved, well into her 90's. Dominick loved to spin silly tales for the grandchildren. Dominick and Mary were positive, fun loving, honest, brave, and hardworking. Dominick Mc Grail died Oct 27, 1979 Worcester, Massachusetts. His wife Mary Heraty McGrail died May 23, 2001.

DONATED 6/6/2016 BY DAUGHTER GRAINNE (GRONYA) MCGRAIL BORN IN WORCESTER, MASS LIVES IN NEW BERN, NORTH CAROLINA RETIRED ELEMENTARY SCHOOL TEACHER, MARRIED.

Bridget Snee

born 8/15/1845
Kilkelly, County Mayo Ireland
Parents: James Snee 1810-1899, Margaret McQuinn 1810

BRIDGET (BIDDY) SNEE IMMIGRATED TO America with her Father, two sisters, Ann and Mary and her two brothers James and Patrick in 1861. It was a voyage that took six weeks to cross the Atlantic Ocean. They arrived in the port of Boston, Massachusetts and they settled in Sudbury, Mass.

In 1861 Bridget met Patrick Brennan, who was a farmer born in 1837 from County Sligo, Ireland. They had come over on the same sailing ship. Bridget and Patrick married on 10/4/1863 in Framingham, Mass. and had nine children, James B-1864, Thomas b-1865, John b-1867, Charles b-1869, infant b/d 1871, Mark b-1873, Katherine b-1875, Richard b-1878, and Margaret b-1880. Patrick found work in the construction industry, carrying the hod, which was a box like implement on a wooden pole to be filled with wet mortar and carried on one's shoulder up the scaffolding to the place where the bricklayers would be working.

In 1873 Patrick and Bridget moved the family to Washington County, Minnesota and they secured a little farm of their own in the newly developed land of Minnesota. They rented a farm for a year or two near Colby's Lake in Woodbury Township. The land was fertile there and the distance to the bustling new city of St. Paul was not very far. The land was all new and not subject to erosion, the amount of wheat that could be grown upon an acre was fantastically more than could be grown on an acre of the stony ground they had known in Ireland, so that for a few years, they were comparatively prosperous.

In 1899 Bridget's father James Snee died in Ireland. In 1900, Brennan family moved to Denmark, Washington County, Minnesota.

Bridget's husband Patrick Brennan dies of acute bronchitis Jan 10, 1912 and on Oct 17, 1914 Bridget Snee Brennan died of diabetes. They were buried together at St. Elizabeth Ann Seton Catholic Cemetery in Hastings, Dakota County, Minnesota.

DONATED 3/26/2016 BY GR GRANDSON PETER LANGENFELD LIVES IN HASTINGS, MINNESOTA, HIS IS A SECURITY OFFICER MARRIED, 1 DAUGHTER

Jeremiah Darby Mee

born 9/6/1886
Glenamaddy, County Galway, Ireland
Parents: Dermott Mee, Bridget Kinahen

JEREMIAH JOSEPH MEE WAS BORN Dermott, after his Father and was called Darby most of his life. He grew up working on his parent's land but at the age of 18 years he left home with his sister Ellen. They left Ireland to Liverpool, England, where they would board a ship headed to New York, in America.

Darby had $15.00 and was planning to work as a laborer and Ellen had $10.00 and planned to work as a servant. They purchased their tickets and missed getting on the ship. So, the next week they had to register for the next available ship to America. On May 5, 1904 Jeremiah and Ellen set out this time with $5.00 and $5.25 respectively. The difference was from having to purchase another ticket to Board, a ship as well as their lodgings. They did not have enough money to purchase two tickets, so as they stood in line Darby went first and got the ticket punched. Then he moved his arm to his back as if he was putting the ticket in his pocket. Ellen took the ticket, placed her hand over the punched hole and she presented the ticket to the Steward, who never saw the previous punched hole. Now both boarded the ship S.S. Teunonic, headed for America, where they would meet, their sister Catherine, who live in St. Louis, Missouri.

Upon arriving in America Darby changed his name and became Jeremiah. Arriving in New York, he found work for a while but became restless. He left to go out West and ended up in Jordan Montana, where he stayed for about 1 year. Then Jeremiah joined the U.S. Army in 1918 and became part of the Wild West Division.

On Nov 7,1918, Ellen received a telegram that her brother Jeremiah was killed in Action. Two weeks later she received a letter from her brother stating he was injured but doing OK. After his recovery, Jeremiah went back East and settled in Chicago, Illinois, where he got a job on the Railroad. It was here he was introduced thru a co-worker to Mary Spaulding.

Mary Spaulding was born Sept 9, 1897 in Lafayette Ave, Chicago, Illinois. She was the daughter of Thomas Spaulding and Mary Jenette Rogers. Mary's Mother died in childbirth and her father, Thomas who worked for the Railroad, was unable to care for a new baby. He gave Mary up to her Maternal Grandfather and aunts to be raised. They sent her to a boarding school.

Jeremiah and Mary married on Aug 24,1921 at St. Margaret Catholic Church in Chicago, Ill. They moved to Cleveland, Ohio and had 5 children. In Cleveland, Jeremiah worked for the Illuminating Company as well as moving from house to house, flipping and restoring them. He eventually settled in Strongsville, Ohio on a farm where he grew crops and had livestock. Here, he was, able to have weekly picnics with the family and his grandchildren.

Jeremiah Darby Mee died Jan 13, 1970 in Parma, Ohio of Cancer. His wife Mary Spaulding Mee died on May 20, 1963 in Warrensville Heights, Cuyahoga, Ohio of Diabetes.

DONATED 7/27/2016 BY GRANDDAUGHTER SARAH KOHLMORGAN
BORN IN CLEVELAND, OHIO, LIVES IN WICKLIFFE, OHIO
MARRIED, 1 DAUGHTER, 1 SON
WORKS FOR AKRON CHILDREN'S HOSPITAL, MENTAL HEALTH TECH.

Patrick Grady

born 2/11/1873
Lecarrow, Clare Island, County Mayo, Ireland
Parents: Patrick William Grady 1841-1911,
Elizabeth Winters 1851-1911

THE GRADY FAMILY LIVED ON the mountainous Clare Island, which guards the entrance to Clew Bay on the West Coast of County Mayo, Ireland. It is the famous home of the Pirate Queen Grainne O'Malley. Also, the famous Lighthouse, established by John Denis Brown, the 1st Marquis of Sligo, built in 1806.

Patrick Grady was the eldest of nine children. He was a Farmer and Blacksmith as his Father was before him. The Grady's grew grain to pay the rent and grew potatoes to feed themselves.

In 1830 the Freedom to Worship Act was invoked in Ireland. Although it was frowned upon to be Catholic in Ireland. Catholics where not allowed to own property. The Grady's attended Sacred Heart Parish, which is still on the Island today. For many year's this church had no Priest. The Priest would come from the near Island of Innisturk to say Mass and give the Sacraments.

The name Grady was originally O'Grady but the O was dropped years before. Patrick's grandchildren would later add the O back onto the name.

Patrick met and married Catherine (Kate) Flanagan. Kate Flanagan was born in 1875, in Strake, Clare Island, Kigeever, and the daughter of James Flanagan and Bridget Cannon. They married in 1901 in the

Catholic Parish Church on Clare Island and they had ninechildren. Patrick died in 1956 at the age of 83 years on Clare Island, County Mayo Ireland

Donated 4/2/2016 by Granddaughter Cecilia Turner
Born in San Francisco, Calif, lives in St. Helena, Calif, Napa Valley Wine Country
Married, 4 children, 5 grandchildren

Katherine Celia Smyth

born 1857
County Longford, Ireland
Parents: Eugene Smyth, Honoria Newman

KATHERINE SMYTH WAS ALREADY 23, and hadn't married because she was the oldest and had been expected to stay and help. She was also in love with a second cousin Thomas Eugene Newman and her parents didn't approve of their relationship. The Newman's family had worked with horses for generations in County Longford.

In 1880 Katherine and Thomas married, they then left Ireland on a Tall Ship for America. They landed in New York City, New York. In New York, Thomas found work as a horse trainer for the Vanderbilt Family. It was on Dec 23, 1890 that Thomas was working with a horse and it kicked him in The head and he died. This was before Workman's Compensation, and the Vanderbuilts gave the Newman Family nothing for Thomas's death.

Katherine was widowed at the age of 33 with five young children, including an infant, and was pregnant at the time. She took in laundry to support herself and her children, and eventually her grandchildren. She never remarried, though she had lots of offers. Her life revolved around her children and her church. She was an excellent seamstress and often made altar linens and vestments for the priests. The only help she would accept was from the County Longford Association. Katherine was a woman of incredible strength. She had an incredible singing voice and she spoke Gaelic when she prayed. She didn't think God would listen to prayers in English.

By 1928 at the age of 71 years, Katherine could no longer continue to do Laundry. In 1935 she became very frail and was diagnosed with Cancer. Catherine Smyth Newman died in Jan 1936.

Donated 8/16/2016 by Granddaughter
 Catherine Ann Curry Mardon
Born Oklahoma City, Oklahoma, Lives in Edmonton, Alberta,
 Canada
Married, Retired Attorney, 2 adopted adult children
Several former adult foster children

John Pickett

born 1837
Ballysheelin, Trinity, County Wexford Ireland
Parents: Samuel Pickett, Hannah Pickett

1841 HANNAH PICKETT TOOK HER son John and fled Ireland. She was 49 years old and John was 4 years They escaped to Liverpool, England because more than half of the Pickett family were arrested, imprisoned, and transported to Australia as political prisoners. From England, Hannah, and her son immigrated to America in 1849 and settled in Rhode Island.

John Pickett served in the military in 1850 in Providence, Rhode Island. He listed in a Seaman's lodging at the age of 13 as a Mariner. Working on ships out of Philadelphia and New York, probably as a cabin boy or deck hand. He served in the military in 1856 at the age of 19 as a Mariner, in Philadelphia, Pennsylvania, and yet again in New York in 1858 at the age of 21.

At the age of 28 years John met Bridget Maher. Bridget was born in 1833, County Cork, Ireland, she was the daughter of Daniel Maher and Mary Carroll. Her name was pronounced as "Mah-Her".

John and Bridget married in 1865 in Philadelphia, Pennsylvania and then quickly moved on to Milford Ohio to farm. In response to the Cherokee Strip Land run of 1893, they moved to Caldwell, Kansas to take part in the free land for homesteader programs.

After the Civil War, because the Cherokee Nation had supported and fought for the Confederacy, the federal government demanded a new treaty made. Land hungry settlers viewed the cattlemen's use of the area as a waste of fertile farmland and pressured the government to purchase the Cherokee land from the Cherokee. Congress eventually paid more than 8-and-a-half-million dollars, or $1.40 per acre, and announced the opening of the Outlet to homesteaders. President Grover Cleveland designated September 16, 1893, as the date for the "run" on 6,000,000 acres. At precisely twelve noon on September 16, 1893 a cannon's boom unleashed the largest land rush America ever saw.

1893 to take part in the free land for homesteader programs, John made the Run into the Cherokee Strip from Caldwell Kansas, staking a claim about 4 miles South of there, and two miles East.

The Irish collection of families from this Land Run now began to improve life. The people are petitioning the Catholic Diocese for a Catholic Church, close to the Irish settlements. They built a church building, with a 15 foot high concrete cross in the middle of the area, keeping it white washed to stand out as a beacon for all to see, and eventually after one of the Fagean Matriarchs in the area, donated 5 acres of land to Bishop Meerschart for the purpose, a church was granted and services began. One of the first marriages was John's son, Robert Jeremiah Pickett & Mary Jane McGuire. They had eight children in fifteen years.

Small county schools sprang up about the same time around the farms, Also, to provide education to the children. John's son, Robert Fredrick Pickett, was born in Renfrow Village, 4 miles west of the church. Medford residents, 7 miles west of the church, and three south, began to grow quickly, as the town was at the intersection of two main highways that service a wider area for agriculture, and it had the Rock Island railroad going through its town, the same railroad that ran south from Caldwell, Kansas. Also, US highway 81 and State highway 11 crossed in the middle of Medford, Oklahoma Territory, and the inevitable happened.

It became intolerable to them to travel the distance to attend church services in the country over dirt roads. The Catholic Diocese moved the church into Medford, Oklahoma, over the strenuous objections of the parishioners that built the church, and moved the services and even some of the buried Irish into a "New St Mary's" parish, and the "new St Mary's' cemetery" west of the original along US 81 Highway, between Renfrow, and Medford Oklahoma. Many of the Irish, who had someone buried at the old cemetery refused to move their relatives, including both John Picket and the McGuire family. They held deep beliefs that their dead relatives, parents, cousins were properly buried in consecrated ground, and digging them up for the convenience of Medford residents was very wrong. Both families, the McGuire's, and the Pickett's graves still are at the original locations close by the homesteads.

On Oct 14,1904 John Pickett partitioned for Naturalization, to be admitted as a citizen of America. John Pickett died 1907 in Fairview Township, Grant Oklahoma. His wife Bridget Maher Pickett died 1907 and is buried next to her husband in the old St. Mary's Cemetery.

DONATED 8/20/2016 BY GR GRANDSON ROBERT PICKETT
BORN IN CALDWELL, KANSAS, LIVES IN MIDWEST CITY, OKLAHOMA
RETIRED POLICE OFFICER

George Evans Lowe

born 8/4/1894
County Galway, Ireland
Parents: Thomas Lowe 1863-1987,
Elizabeth Evan 1867- 1895

GEORGE LOWE WAS 6 MONTHS old when his mother died. George was sent to live with his Maternal Grandmother, Susan Evans, in Hollymount, County Mayo Ireland, as his father had to go to work. His father was with the Royal Irish Constabulary (Police Force) and unable to look after George. When he got older, George was sent to a boy's school in Ranelagh, Athlone, County Westmeath, Ireland.

In 1913 at the age of 18 years, George left Ireland to go to Liverpool, England to board the ship S.S. Dominion which took him to Halifax, Nova Scotia. From Nova Scotia, he went to Gladstone, Manitoba, Canada where he stayed at the boarding house of Robert and Elizabeth Vinie. Here George met the Vinie's daughter Annie Ellen Vinie, whom he made friends with, and she was just 16 years old.

On Jan 7,1916, he joined the Canadian Over-Seas Expeditionary Force and fought with the Canadians in WWI. In 1919 George shipped back to Gladstone, Manitoba, Canada where he reconnected his friendship with Annie Ellen Vinie. Annie was born March 21,1900 in Gladstone, Manitoba And was the daughter of Robert Vinie and Elizabeth Ann Grantham.

George and Annie married on Dec 29, 1920. Annie was a Teacher until she married and had her five children, Dorothy Elizabeth, Robert

Evans, twins, George Vinie and Georgina Mae, and Lawrence James. George was now a farmer.

George's father died in Ireland on March 6, 1930 and George never went back to Ireland to see him. In 1941 the family moved to Winnipeg, Manitoba, Canada, and George went to work with the Canadian Corp of Commissionaires and he retired after 27 years on June 1, 1968 with the rank of Division Sergeant Major.

On Nov 13, 1973, George's wife, Annie Ellen Vinie Lowe died in Winnipeg, Manitoba, Canada. George Lowe died on Jan 30, 1983 and was buried next to his wife.

DONATED 8/22/2016 BY GRANDDAUGHTER GEORGINA LOWE NELSON
BORN IN STONEWALL, MANITOBA, CANADA. LIVES IN TREULON, MANITOBA
MARRIED, RETIRED, TWINS, 1 BOY, DECEASED, 1 GIRL LIVING,

Ellen Marie (Nellie) Leahy

born 1874
Gortnamona Parish, Schull, County West Cork, Cork
Ireland
Parents: James Leahy, Bridget Sullivan

IN 1890 NELLIE LEAHY LEFT Ireland and headed for San Francisco, California. Her father had arranged a marriage for her to a much older man, which she wanted no part of. Nellie decided to head off to America where she had a a couple of Aunts that lived in, San Francisco, California. Nellie broke into her father's strong box and took enough money for steerage aboard a ship.

Steerage was the lower part of the ship where cargo was stored. Immigrants that were too poor to afford to travel on the upper decks got to be stuffed into converted cargo spaces. This was the lowest class of travel.

When Nellie's father found out what Nellie had done, he gave her additional money for the voyage. He would not allow his daughter to travel in Steerage. Sadly, Nellie never saw her parents again. Nellie was one of eight children and several of her siblings did later join her in America.

In 1893, after travelling across America, Nellie finally arrived in San Francisco, California, where there was a very large Irish Community, and where her Aunt lived. In San Francisco, Nellie met Patrick O'Brien.

Patrick was from a neighboring town of Ballydehob, back in County Cork, Ireland. Patrick was a Teamster and drove a Beer Truck. They married and had three children, Marie, Jimmy, and Evelyn. In 1900 they lived at Minna St. south of the Market area. Along with Nellies husband Patrick and her children, Jimmy and Evelyn, Patrick's sister Kate has come to live with them as well as Nellie's sisters Mame and Kate. Nellie's daughter Marie died as a young child.

In 1901 Patrick died from a work related, accident on the Beer Truck, which was a very dangerous job. Left to take care of her children after Patrick died, Nellie opened a saloon which was very prosperous for her. Alcohol companies contracted the Irish to sell liquor. This was during Prohibition and many proponents of Prohibition were also a very Ant-Irish.

All this changed very fast in 1906. San Francisco was hit with a very large earthquake and fire. Nellie's home and business was dynamited as a fire break to help stop the raging fire. Nellie had made a very good living with the Saloon and she had saved enough money with the intent to take her children back to Ireland to visit her family. But had to sell the tickets due to the earthquake and fire.

At this, time, Nellie had a new suitor she had been seeing by the name of Denis Rogers. Denis had commandeered a wagon and ran inside the Saloon to save what he could and he grabbed many personal items, clothing, pictures, and a clock. This act endeared him closer to Nellie. With all the items that Denis, was able, to save, they then traveled to Golden Gate Park to camp out for a while.

First, they move to 24th St, where all the working class, Irish lived after the earthquake. Nellie then found work for a large laundry and later when her daughter Evelyn turned 14 years old, she also worked in the laundry. Denis and her son Jimmy found work as caddies. When they had saved enough money, they bought a house on San Jose Ave. in the Ocean view area.

Years later, Nellie's daughter, Evelyn meets a very nice man named Joe Sutherland and they marry and have two girls, making Nellie a very happy Grandma.

In the late 1930's Nellie is in her 60's and she lets a neighborhood bootlegger store his moonshine in the basement of her house. The Police found out and both Nellie and Denis were arrested and taken out of the house still in their slippers. Joe Sutherland is related to half of the Police force and knows most of the men in the other half of the force, so they are released and nothing came of it.

Ellen Marie Leahy Rogers died in 1944 and was buried at Holy Cross Cemetery in San Francisco, California and was buried with both her Husbands, her baby Marie, and son Jimmy.

DONATED 8/23/2016 BY GREAT GRANDDAUGHTER VALERIE MCGREW
BORN IN SAN FRANCISCO, CALIFORNIA, LIVES IN DALY CITY, SUBURB OF SAN FRANCISCO
WIDOW, 1 SON IAN, WHO PASSED AWAY
VOLUNTEER LIBRARIAN AT THE UNITED IRISH CULTURE CENTER IN SAN FRANCISCO, CALIF

Catherine (Kitty) Cochrane

born 1821
Buncrana, County Donegal, Northern Ireland
Parents: Joseph Cochran 1789-1865, Rebecca Orr

CATHERINE COCHRANE WAS THE YOUNGEST daughter of Joseph and Rebecca Cochran. Catherine left Ireland to travel to Gravesend, England on Oct 19, 1851, her brother, Joseph, accompanying her as far as London, England. Here she boarded the Ship S.S. Katherine Stewart Forbes for her journey to New Zealand.

Catherine's voyage was to be a lengthy one and the Katharine Stewart Forbes being well overdue by the time it reached New Zealand. Catherine's passage was paid for by Thomas Mackey, whom she knew in Ireland.

Thomas Mackey had left Ireland in 1848 to go to New Zealand and the pair had been corresponding since the time of Thomas's departure for New Zeland.

In February 1849 Thomas Macky wrote to Catherine (known as Kitty), *"It is with feeling of no ordinary kind that I now sit down to write to you with the recollection of the many happy hours I have spent in your society which it is difficult to believe will ever return, when unknown to many we sat together for hours talking of what? No matter, they were happy hours at least to me, and it is now I feel the reality when I have no kind friend to tell all my joys and cares. But why should I despair, heretofore God has ordered all things well for us, and I know He will yet grant me my petition and bring you in safety to this land."*

The bond between the pair came as a surprise to the Macky family. Of, their affection John Macky wrote, *"As reguards, Thomas forming a connection with Miss Cochrane, I never heard a word about it nor ever thought of the like until I received Thomas's first letter. I was not satisfied when I saw the letter, I was taken, by surprise but I can say nothing against Miss Cochrane and if they have made up their minds to be connected, together I have no objection and may God bless and prosper them."*

On their arrival in New Zealand, some of the passengers openly complained about the on-board conditions in the Auckland newspapers. However, Catherine and other passengers found it within themselves to place an advertisement in the *Daily Southern Cross* to thank the captain for *"the strict attention paid to the management of your ship; and, also, the just, kind and gentlemanly manner, in which you have treated us."*

Reunited at last, Thomas and Kitty married within two weeks of her arrival in the St Andrews church, Symonds St, in a ceremony officiated by the Rev. John Inglis. They at first lived in a small cottage off Hobson St. which is now a part of the Auckland CBD before relocating to a brick house in Hobson St opposite the St. Matthews Church (now St. Matthews in the City).

In 1854 two of Catherine's sisters and their families also immigrated to New Zealand. The party of emigrants included Catherine's widowed sister, Ann Alexander, and Rebecca Macky, wife of Thomas's brother, the Rev. John Macky. Their brother, Joseph Cochrane, and the Macky elders also travelled with them. Another brother, Samuel, would follow from Montreal in 1858.

Kitty and Thomas had four children. Their four children, John, Joseph, Sarah and Thomas Jr were born in 1853, 1855, 1856 and 1858. Sadly, their oldest, John, died as a baby in February 1855, not long before the birth of their second child, Joseph Cochrane Macky. However, Catherine's health deteriorated markedly following the birth of her youngest child and despite being under constant medical supervision and care from her sister, Rebecca, Catherine finally departed this world on 1st December, 1859.

An entry from her brother-in-law, the Rev. John Macky's journal of same date, describes the family's sorrow: *"This evening was very lowering and already raining and there was no meeting. I returned home and came into my study where I was not seated more than a few minutes when a messenger arrived from Auckland with the overwhelming intelligence of my dear sister-in-law Kitty's death. Oh, the bitter, bitter grief I shall never forget the anguish of this hour. So, unexpected that I was even blaming her for keeping my own dear wife so long from home! Oh! God forgive every unkind thought which may have passed through my mind of that kind, loving heart which now beats no longer."*

Reverend Macky rode to Auckland the following morning, where he assisted at Kitty's post mortem. *"I needn't dwell on the sad meetings of this day and its bursting grief"*, he said adding that *"it was melancholy satisfaction to know that no human skill could have averted the sad calamity."*

Kitty's remains were interred the following day at the Symonds St Cemetery as the family, deep in their own grief, gathered around her bereft husband, Thomas Macky.

DONATED 7/8/2016 BY GR GREAT GRANDNIECE WANDA HOPKINS
BORN AUCKLAND, NEW ZEALAND, LIVES IN ADELAIDE HILLS, SOUTH
  AUSTRALIA
OFFICE MANAGER, LIVES WITH HER PARTNER GRAHAM. 2 CHILDREN

Martin Neary

born 1/1842
Kilroy, Parish of Aughrim, County Roscommon, Ireland
Parents: John Neary, Sarah Conlon

IN 1864 MARTIN NEARY EMIGRATED from Ireland on the ship S.S. Morning Star headed for Australia. He boarding the ship under his brother's name, Peter Neary, as he was involved in the Irish Brotherhood. But as soon as he left the ship Martin used his own name from then on. Martin was a very good singer and many time while aboard ship he was invited to the Captain's Cabin to entertain the 1st and 2nd class guests. Aboard the same ship was fellow passenger Eleanor Sharkey, whom he met and later married. Ellen Sharkey was born in 1845 in Elphin, County Roscommon, Ireland, a nearby village to where Martin lived.

On Sept 6 1864, the ship S.S. Morning Star arrived in Australia and Martin went mining for gold and he found gold. With the money from his gold Martin bought 6 Pubs, one of his Pubs, called the Revolving Battery is still a bar in Sydney today, But It's now called The Old Fitzroy.

Martin and Eleanor married and had seven children. In 1865 Martin brought his brother-in-Law Lawrence Sharkey over from Ireland to help manage the Pubs, where Martin was unable to manage them. Instead of helping Martin and Eleanor, Lawrence embezzled a lot of the Pubs money and ran off to Western Australia with one of the parlor maids from Martin's Pub. On one occasion, Martin tried to stop a runaway carriage and in the process, he got kicked in the face by the horse. Upon seeing Martins bloody face, his wife Eleanor took a stroke and died on April 16,

1888. She was buried at Waverley Cemetery in Sydney. Martin went on running his pubs. Martin Neary died on Nov 3, 1907 and was buried with his wife in the family crypt at Waverley Cemetery in Sydney, Australia.

In 2015, eighty of Martin Neary's direct descendants had a reunion at Martin and Eleanor's Pub in Wooloomooloo, Australia.

Donated on 9/1/2016 by Great Grandson Paul Lawrence Neary
Born in Sydney, NSW, Australia, lives in Newcastle, NSW, Australia
Currently working in Doha, Qatar, Single, 1 daughter, Sian Neary

Katherine Flanagan

born 5/11/1873
Moate, County Westmeath, Ireland
Parents: Patrick Flanagan 1837-1931,
Ellen Coady 1841-1908

PATRICK FLANAGAN AND HIS BROTHER Michael come from Ballymore and started the Flanagan dynasty and established a Saw Mill and joinery Works in Moate, with branches in Ballinasloe and in Mullingar. They employed fifty people, manufacturing furniture, coffins, and farm machinery. The Coady family were builders, stonemasons, bricklayers, and farmers.

Patrick Flanagan's first son, Michael Flanagan [1869-1930], and the next son to be married, Patrick Flanagan [1876-1944], managed the mills in Ballinasloe and in Mullingar. Katherine was not in line to inherit any of the family sawmills.

Katherine was sent to Edinburgh for nursing training where she met her future husband, Richard Patrick Stuart Brown. Richard was born March 1, 1873 in Edinburgh, Scotland and was the son of Richard Stuart Brown and Janet Rodger. Richard went home with Katherine to Ireland for Christmas to meet the family, but in those days, they needed to travel with a chaperone. Richard's sister Roberta travelled with them, and when they arrived in Moate at Katherine's home, Roberta met Katherine's older brother Michael Flanagan. Both couples were married in Ireland.

Michael stayed in Ireland with his new wife Roberta, as manager of one of the sawmills. Katherine and Richard emigrated to Canada around 1903 and settled in Calgary, Alberta, Canada where they raised seven children. Richard took a job in the Government and was a customs official for the Government of Canada in Calgary Alberta. Times were not always easy, and during the Depression, Katherine became known for making Champagne from potatoes. Richard also, developed a drinking problem as many of the Irish do. At one point Katherine went home to Ireland, but was told by her parents to go back to Canada. You married him, deal with it! Life went on.

Katherine's husband Richard died in early 1951 in Calgary, Alberta at age 77. Katherine Flanagan Brown died July 24, 1951 in Vancouver, British Columbia at age 78.

DONATED 9/6/2016 BY GRANDSON GEORGE BROWN.
BORN IN CALGARY, ALBERTA, LIVES IN OTTAWA, CANADA.
10 YEARS WITH THE INTERNATIONAL STAFF AT NATO HEADQUARTERS IN BRUSSELS, BELGIUM.
HIS WIFE WAS KILLED IN A CAR ACCIDENT, REMARRIED, RETIRED, 2 CHILDREN AND FOUR GRANDCHILDREN,

James Carlile McCoan

born 7/14/1829
Dunlow, County Tyrone, Northern Ireland
Parents: Clement McCoan, Sarah Carlile

JAMES CARLILE MCCOAN WAS AN only child of Clement and Sarah McCoan. He was educated at Dungannan School and Homerton College in London, England. He enrolled at London University in 1848 and he became a Barrister in London.

James became deeply engaged in Journalism and was a War Correspondent for the "Daily News" during the Crimean War. At the end of the War he travelled to and settled in Constantinople, Istanbul, as a Supreme Court Consulor till 1864.

On June 2,1857, he married Augusta Janet Jenkyns. She was the youngest daughter of William Jenkyns of Elgin. They had one son and one daughter, Amy Georgina, both were born in Istanbul.

James became the Editor of the first English Newspaper in Turkey, "The Livant Herald". In 1870 he and his family returned to England where he lived at Kensington Square, in London, where he wrote several books: Egypt Under Ismail, and Our New Protectorate: Turkey in Asia.

In 1880-1885 James represented Wicklow County, Ireland as a Protestant Home-Ruler in Parliament. He worked for the Independence of Ireland.

James's daughter Amy Georgina was married in St. Mary's Church in Kensington in 1902.

James Calile MCCoan died on Jan 13, 1904 at his home in Kensington Square and was buried at Kensal Green, London, England. He died two weeks before his daughter Amy Georgina gave birth to his grandson, James George, McCoan Bellewes, whom he longed so much to see.

DONATED 9/10/2016 BY GR GRANDDAUGHTER MARY FARMER
BORN ROCHFORD ESSEX, ENGLAND, LIVES IN EASTBOURNE, E SUSSEX
WORKED AS A MED LAB TECH, RETIRED, MARRIED, 2 CHILDREN

James McDonald

born 11/24/1883
Crover, Broomfield, County Monaghan Ireland
Parents: Peter McDonnell, Brigid Burns

JAMES MCDONALD WAS THE ELDEST of four children of Peter and Brigid McDonnell. Both his parents were illiterate and they lived on a small piece of allotment of Land where his father was a tenant farmer.

In 1901 James left the family home in Ireland and moved to England to find work. In 1903 James purchased a third class, steamship ticket at a princely sum of 17 pounds sterling, at the Port of London and boarded the ship S.S. Rimutaka headed for Wellington, New Zealand. His rations of for the voyage consisted of potatoes, dried peas, lime juice, beef, coffee, tea and twenty-one quarts of water.

By the time, he arrived at Wellington, New Zealand, James had changed from McDonnell to McDonald. James obtained a job at a local Hotel, "The Cambridge" where his job was to roll barrels of beer into the basement of the Hotel. After a few years he took a job at the "Albert Hotel". This Hotel was known as the "Old Identities" as from about 1880 the exterior walls of the Hotel had been decorated with sculpted heads of early pioneer notables.

James was a very industrious man and he had a very strong desire to improve himself. James hired a tutor to help him gain an accomplishment of the basics of reading, writing, and mathematics. His self-education together with his ambition to improve his station had returned remarkable results.

By 1910 James had become the proprietor of the "Albert Hotel" and as a licensed Victualler in a small colonial city he had gained a degree of respectability.

James had met Evelyn Murphy, who was born in Wellington, New Zealand. Her grandfather, Owen Murphy, had arrived in New Zealand in 1861, as a Sergeant in the 65th Regiment of the British Imperial Forces during the period of land Wars. Evelyn had attended St. Mary's Girls College in Wellington and was a very intelligent and beautiful woman. They married in 1911 and had four children; James, Mary, Peter, and Thomas.

James was not a very religious person but he did believe that the education offered by the Catholic Schools was superior. Therefore, enroll his children into Catholic schools.

In 1920 James brother. Peter arrived from Ireland and James looked after him, providing Peter with employment and accommodations. Peter had left his wife and daughter back in Ireland with the intent to make his fortune before returning to Ireland. But Peter never did return and in 1955 he died of cancer in Wellington. James provided monetary support to Peter's wife and daughter for the rest of his life, which included when the bank threatened to foreclose on Peter's home in Castleblayney, County Monaghan Ireland, James paid the Mortgage.

James developed an association with the local racing fraternity and he held various official offices within the Wellington Trotting Club, including for many years the appointment of Club Steward. Over this period, James also owned at least 2 race horses. One of which, "Grey Lady" won a Provincial Cup in 1930. James was also drawn into local politics becoming a Wellington City counsellor for a single term.

The Albert Hotel thrived under James until it was sold in 1923, it was later demolished to make way for a new hotel. It was around this time that James commissioned the building of a three story, office block next to the new hotel that had replaced the Albert Hotel. The new building was called "McDonald Building" and remained in the family until 1968. The McDonald Building marked The beginning of a career as a landlord in which over three decades he acquired and sold numerous properties around Wellington. After he sold the hotel the family settled into a spacious single level dwelling with a large section near to the city center. Evelyn's younger spinster sister, Aileen, was a full time resident and it was Aileen, who actually ran the household. Evelyn's deteriorating health prevented her from carrying out any of the traditional home making duties. James daughter Mary, died in1950 at the age of 36 from Polio Meningitis. His son Peter died in 1988, having suffered from Post-Traumatic Stress Disorder as a result of his experience as a POW in Germany during WW II.

Thomas James, youngest son was a recluse. His son James went to University becoming a Doctor and was a source of great pride to James.

James taught his grandchildren that hard work would invariably bring rewards. To reinforce this maxim, James paid his grandchildren when they mowed the lawn, tended the vegetable garden or drove him where he needed to go. James never learned to drive.

James McDonald was a very kind and generous man with a mischief humor. He once acquired a whiskey tumbler with a small hole drilled just below the lip of the glass. When drinking from the glass, the spirits would dribble, down the front of the recipient shirt. James thought that such pranks were very hilarious.

In 1960 James, did make a trip back to Ireland. He died in 1968 at the age of 84 years.

DONATED 9/1/2016 BY GRANDSON PATRICK MCDONALD
BORN IN LONDON, ENGLAND, RETIRED NEW ZEALAND ARMY OFFICER
MARRIED, 2 DAUGHTERS, 3 GRANDSONS

John Church

born 1871
Loughguile, Country Antrim, Northern Ireland
Parents: John Church, Elizabeth McGoogan

JOHN CHURCH AND LIZZIE MCVEIGH were married on April 3, 1894 at St. Patrick & St. Brigid Catholic Church, in the small town of Ballycastle, County Antrim, Northern Ireland. Ballycastle is located on the Northeast coast of Ireland.

Elizabeth (Lizzie) McViegh was born in 1868 and was the daughter of Patrick McVeigh and Mary Mc Cambridge, and was from Cregganboy, Ballycastle, County Antrim.

After being married only six weeks they decided to emigrate from Ireland to America. Leaving Ireland from Moville, Country Donegal on the Ship S.S. "City of Rome", they arrived in New York City, New York on May 21, 1894. They headed to rural Wayne County in the northeast corner of Pennsylvania where Lizzie had family.

John got a job working for the Ontario & Western Railroad. The railroad rented living space above the stations to employees. They lived above the station in Pleasant Mt. Pennsylvania where their son John was born. Their first five children were born in Pennsylvania, James, Mary, John, Rose, and Daniel. John worked at night and Lizzie was alone with the children. She was lonely and wanted to go home to Ireland.

In 1900 they did just that. They left from Philadelphia, Pennsylvania and headed back to Ireland with their children. When they reached Ireland they quickly found that there was no work. John's brother Patrick had gone to Scotland in search of work while John and Lizzie were in America. Patrick told his brother John that he would have no problem finding work in Scotland. The family left Ireland for Scotland and John found work in Greenock, which is in the north western lowland part of Scotland. John and Lizzie had seven more children, Francis, Jean, Archibald, Ann, Charles, Hugh, and George.

In 1930 John and Lizzie return to America on the ship S.S. Cameronia. Three of the older boys, two of whom were married and had children by this time decided to stay in Scotland. All the other children headed to America with the parents. The family settled in Brooklyn, New York. John and Lizzie never owned a home, they always rented. John was a very tall man, over 6ft who had a good job as a doorman at the Park Plaza Hotel in New York City for many years. He used to let his grandson George sit on his lap and play with his mustache. John Church passed away in 1955 at the age of 83years. His wife Elizabeth (Lizzie) Church passed away in 1961 at the age of 93years.

DONATED 9/16/2016 BY GRANDSON GEORGE CHURCH
BORN IN BROOKLYN, NEW YORK, LIVES IN SMITHTOWN LONG ISLAND, NEW YORK
MARRIED, RETIRED, ONE SON, THREE GRANDSONS

Gavin Shaw

born 6/21/1813
Glenanne, Loughgilly, County Armagh, Northern Ireland

GAVIN SHAW STARTED WORKING FOR Glenanne Linen Mills at the age of 22 years in 1835. He met Susannah Gass, who was from the neighboring town of Tullyallen, County Armagh, 45 miles to the south of Loughgilly, County Armagh. Sarah was born Jan 11, 1819, and was the daughter of Benjamin Gass and Rachel Porter of Tulyallen. They married in 1839 and lived on a 7, acre lease of land next to Shaw Lake in Glenanne. Gavin and Susannah had seven children, all born in Ireland; Gavin 1840, Benjamin 1841, Elizabeth 1844, William John 1847, Raheal 1848, Robert 1851 and Susannah 1854.

In the early part of 1850 Gavin made two trips to America to visit Susannah two brothers living in Pennsylvania, Robert, and John Gass. Robert and John advised Gavin to immigrate to Canada. In 1855 Gavin gave up his job of 20years in the Linen Mills, leased out his 7acres of land and, made, arrangements for his family to immigrate to Canada. Gavin and his family boarded a ship from Belfast, Northern Ireland. His family stood by the deck rail of the ship as they sailed out into the ocean until they could no longer see land. Their trip was a six week voyage to arrive at Canada. Their ship sailed up the St. Lawrence River to Montreal, where Susannah had a sister Mary, that they would stay with.

Many weeks went by and the gold sovereigns Gavin had received for the Lease of his land began to dwindle down. His sovereigns were carried in a belt worn around his waist. When he wanted money Gavin just untied the belt and cut off a sovereign. And his belt was very heavy.

It was very difficult for Gavin to find work in Montreal because he did not speak French. He did find work on road construction which he was unprepared for. Gavin was well educated in Mathematics and could speak Latin but he never did manual labor and was not mechanically inclined. He never even learned to hoe a hill of potatoes or chop fire wood and he came home with very little wages.

In 1856 one of Susannah's brothers came to visit from America. He told Gavin that here was to be held an examination for Teachers Certificates and advised Gavin to take the exam. Gavin took the exam and obtained a permit to teach on June 8 1856. He then moved his family to Port Hope Ontario and very soon he was established in a school near Port Hope with a yearly salary of $400.

In 1860 the Indian land of Sarawak and Keppel was, opened, to settlers. Gavin dispatched his oldest son Gavin, then 20years old, to obtain land. Gavin obtained a lot on the 17th concession of Keppel. This 17th concession of Keppel, below the line stone hills, should have been called a blind line, for to this day, the western exit, is barred by a formidable rock hill. Gavin moved his family from Port Hope to Keppel, twelve miles North of Owen Sound. His sons Gavin and Benjamin went to work building a log house and clearing the land. Gavin Shaw died in 1892 at the age of 79 years old. His wife Susannah Gass Shaw died in 1906 and they were buried in Greenwood Cemetery at Owen Sound, Ontario, Canada.

DONATED 9/18/2016 GR GREAT GRANDSON LARRY JONES
BORN IN WIARTON, ONTARIO, CANADA, LIVES IN PASADINA, NEW
  FOUNDLAND, CANADA
MARRIED, ONE SON, ONE DAUGHTER, RETIRED

Sarah Willis

born 4/8/1821
Newtownbarry, County Wexford, Ireland
Parents: Jacob Willis, Elizabeth Swain

SARAH WILLIS MARRIED MILES HOWELL in 1838 and they had one son James born Aug 3, 1839. Miles Howell born Jan 22, 1819 London, Middlesex, England. They decided they wanted to leave Ireland and go to Victoria Australia.

In 1840 they were about to board the ship S.S. Himalaya (which was bound for Port Phillip Bay Victoria, Australia) when the captain of the ship would not allow baby James aboard the ship. They left their son James with Sarah's parents to raise him until he got older and he could join them in Australia later. James was then raised by Sarah's sister Jane and her husband John Rothwell. Sadly, James never was sent to Australia to join his parents.

Sarah and Miles arrived Sept 30, 1839 in Port Phillip Bay, Melbourne, Australia. Upon arriving Miles found work doing manual labor and some farm work. In 1843, he was employed, by James Atkinson in the coastal town of Port Fairy, Victoria, Australia. James Atkinson was a Sydney solicitor and he purchased land in the town of Port Fairy by special survey. He drained the swamps, subdivided and leased the land. He also built a harbor on the Moyne River. Mr. Atkinson hired Miles to help him survey the land.

In 1861 Miles purchased land in village Orford, in Victoria, Australia, on the East Coast of the Prosser River. He then purchased several Bullock wagons and horse wagons and started his own carrier business. Miles became very well known, and respected in the town. Sarah and Miles lived in Orford about 17 miles from Port Fairy on a farm they named Wattle farm.

Sarah and Miles had several children in Australia; Frances b-1843, William b-1845, Sarah Jane b-1849, Emily b-1850, Miles b-1851, Elizabeth Ann b-1857, Rachel Ross b-1860, Jacob b-1862 and Georgiana who was born 1865.

Miles Howell died of a Heart Attack on April 18, 1889 and his wife Sarah Willis Howell died on Sept 28, 1909. They were buried together in the Port Fairy Public Cemetery, Victoria, Australia.

DONATED ON 9/27/2016 BY GREAT GRAND DAUGHTER, SHARANE LYONS
BORN IN BENTLEIGH EAST, VICTORIA, AUSTRALIA,
  LIVING IN BERWICK, VICTORIA
RETIRED QUALITY CONTROL OFFICER, MARRIED

James Paul Geraghty

born 6/29/1865
County Roscommon Ireland
Parents: Patrick Geraghty, Kate Moran

IN 1895, JAMES GERAGHTY AND his brother, Johnnie left Ireland and took the long voyage to South Africa. They arrived in Algoa Bay, which is a wide inlet along the South African East Coast, east of the Cape of Good Hope.

Having arrived in Algoa Bay, James met Marion Hartford. Her Grandfather was James Hartford, who had fled Ireland during the Great Hunger of 1840 (the so called Famine).

James and his brother Johnnie along with Marion and her sister Margaret travelled north to Transvaal Republic, where James joined John MacBride's Irish Brigade. They fought on the side of the Boers in the Battle of Colenso on December 15, 1899.

The Battle of Colenso was the third and final battle fought during the Black Week of the second Boar War. It was fought, by the British and Boer Forces for the independent South African Republic in Colenso, Natal, South Africa.

In 1897 James married Marion in the Loretto Convent Church in Pretoria, South Africa. While James and Marion lived in Pretoria, he made a living as an Architect and a builder. His oldest brother Johnnie had been killed while working on the Post Office building in Pretoria.

In June 1900, when the British soldiers marched into the City, James took his wife Marion, her sister Margaret and their new born son, Reginald, and fled to Delagoa Bay in Mozambique. From here they caught a boat back to Ireland. If he had stayed and was captured, he would have had to face a firing squad for treason since he fought with the Boers against the British and Ireland was under English occupation.

In 1901, James and Marion had their second son George, who was born in Dublin Ireland. James continued work as an Architect where he designed many buildings in Galway and they are still standing today. Marion's sister, Margaret married James's brother George.

James Paul Geraghty died in 1910 of Pneumonia and was buried in Athleague, County Roscommon, Ireland.

DONATED 10/18/2016 BY GRANDSON TERRENCE PLAYDON, AGE 74
BORN IN PORT ELIZABETH, SOUTH AFRICA, LIVES IN FERNS, COUNTRY WEXFORD, IRELAND
DIVORCED, 2 SONS, 1 DAUGHTER, RETIRED

John Joseph Sheehan

born 4/8/1880
Kielduff Mountain in Ballincullig, Ballymacelligott
Parish, Tralee, County Kerry, Ireland
Parents: Timothy Sheehan, Johanna McArthy

TIMES WERE HARD FOR THE Kerry farmer. The Sheehan farm was a rented, a wee two bedroom, thatched cottage at the bottom of Kielduff Mountain in Ballincullig, same as all the neighbor's.

John Joseph Sheehan was the second of seven children. John, a quiet man, worked as did his brothers and sisters as servants on the neighbor's farms. Faith was and is the foundation of the Sheehan family. Without faith, one could not survive the atrocities committed to the Irish family.

Every summer, all the neighboring families and cousins at Ballincullig and Beheenagh (across the lane) would walk up the mountain to the bog. They would spend days cutting peat for each family's winter needs. Along with singing, dancing and having picnics. Little did they know, that would be passed down to their great grandchildren today.

This was a time when there was no jobs or work in the neighboring town of Tralee and there was not enough food to go around. John's Uncle had already immigrated to America, and he wrote back to the Sheehan family that there was a need for more railroad workers and if they came to Indiana they could find work. It was John's older brother Andrew's duty was to stay and run the family farm.

In 1900 John decided to leave Ireland to find work and traveled to America. At the age of 17 years, he boarded the ship S.S. Lucania and on May 27, 1897 arrived in New York City, New York with only one suitcase. From New York John traveled to his Uncle's home in Fort Wayne, Indiana where his Uncle worked for the Railroad. John acquire a job as a Fireman and later as a Locomotive Engineer for the Pennsylvania Railroad. When he established himself, and saved enough money John financed and sent for his brother Patrick and his two sisters, Mary and Martha to join him. When his brother Patrick arrived, he obtained a job with the Pennsylvania Railroad. When John's sisters, Mary and Martha arrived, they joined, The Order of the Sisters of Providence in Terra Haute, Indiana.

In Indiana John met an Irish-German woman, Bridgid Elizabeth (Lizzy) Kuhn. Lizzy was from Winimac, Indiana. They married and had four children, John Vincent b-Oct 8,1913, George Patrick b-Nov 24,1914, Margaret Elizabeth b-Aug 23,1917, and Mary Ellen b-Dec20,1923.

In 1947, just days after her Wedding Day, daughter Mary Ellen passed away. Shortly after her death, Lizzy Sheehan passed away from a stroke. In 1957 John Joseph Sheehan passed away from a stroke. They are all buried together at the Catholic Cemetery, in Fort Wayne, Indiana.

DONATED 11/9/2016 BY GREAT GRANDDAUGHTER SHELLY SANDS
BORN IN FORT WAYNE, INDIANA, LIVES IN NEWRY, COUNTY DOWN,
    NORTHERN IRELAND
MARRIED, 4 CHILDREN, ISABELLA, ZACHARY, FAITH, AND BRIDGET

Michael Pollard

born 10/1833
Castlepollard, County Westmeath, Ireland

MICHAEL POLLARD AND HIS BROTHER left Ireland in 1851 and traveled to America. They settled in New Jersey where they lived for 5 years. In 1860 he was a laborer on the Lewis Carston farm. In 1861 Michael moved to Illinois where he joined the 9th Illinois Calvary. He enlisted on Sept 1, 1861 and mustered out on Dec 5, 1862.

After the War, Michael met another Irish immigrated, Bridget Maloney. Bridget was born in 1839 in Freakle, County Clare Ireland, the daughter of James William and Bridget Maloney. She came to America at the age of 13 in 1852 on the ship S.S. George Green and arrived in New York City. Bridget was educated and could read and write.

Michael and Bridget married and had 7 children, James b-1863 Mary b-1865, Katie b-1867, Maggie b-1867, Joseph Francis b-1870, John b-1875, Rose b-1876, and Teressa b-1880.

In 1878 they lived in Iowa City, Wright Iowa and Michael was a farmer. All the daughters stayed living in Iowa, two sons, John and James moved to Edmonton, Alberta, Canada, and Joseph moved to Washington State. John and his brother James are bother buried at Mt. Pleasant Cemetery, Edmonton, Alberta Canada. Michael Pollard died in 1913 and he and his wife Bridget Maloney Pollard are buried in a Catholic Cemetery in Grundy Center, Iowa.

Donated 11/4/2016 by Great Grandson John Pollard
Born in Hollywood, California, lives in San Diego, California
Retired Navy, Widowed, 1 son, 1 daughter

Elizabeth "Lizzy" Lennon

born 11/3/1886
Mourne Mountains, County Down, Northern Ireland

ELIZABETH LENNON WAS BORN IN Nov 3,1886 and shortly after her birth, her Mother died. When Lizzy was just 3 years old, her father died and she went to live with her Aunt Rose Sloan.

Perhaps she saw her ticket out of poverty in a marriage to Patrick O'Prey. Patrick was the son of Richard O'Prey 1853-1915 and Ellen McAvoy 1853-1929, born Jan 1879 in Liverpool, England. In 1908, Patrick and Lizzy married in a Catholic Church in Gargary, County Down.

The newlyweds attempted to seek employment in Glasgow, Scotland. Patrick O'Prey found employment as steel worker, laborer, street cleaner, and Sanitation man. Also, while living in Scotland was the birth of Patrick's son, Richard O'Prey was born on March 30, 1910.

In 1912, Patrick O'Prey, decided to join his brothers Peter, Jack, Henry, and Dick in at securing a more predictable life. The five brothers signed up for a mining excursion to the western United States. Each, left relatives, in County Down and emigrated to Park City, Utah where they found work in the lead and zinc mines. They later relocated to the copper mines in Butte, Montana. Although relatively well paid as miners in Montana, few coins found the way back to County Down and into the budget of Lizzie and her infant son, Richard Benedict. Within two years of beginning life in Utah and Montana, Patrick found his mobility severely constricted by the outbreak of World War I. Complementing that cataclysmic event in 1914, the outbreak of the Irish rebellion on

Easter Monday, 1916 generated more complications for the young mother with the toddler son left in County Down without any reliable source of income.

The Sloan family virtually disowned Lizzie when she chose to marry Patrick O'Prey, and the O'Prey in-laws either had too many problems of their own or resented the drain on their minor resources by the presence of another adult mouth to feed and young child to support.

As a young mother, Lizzie was determined to find secure housing for her son and employment for herself. Moving from one slum to another in the area around Belfast, Lizzie sought employment wherever she could. The linen mills of County Down hired women at a lower wage, a few pence higher than the allocation for child labor. She also dug potatoes for a shilling a day, but she thought she found her best job as cook for the Royal Irish Constabulary in Castlewellan. She lost that job when she refused to cook bacon on a Friday for the overwhelmingly Protestant force. She also tried employment at the Slieve Donnard Hotel in Newcastle. It was a posh vacation spot for visiting British and wealthy Protestants from Ulster.

Lizzy enrolled her son in a sequence of schools that achieved remarkable results despite his temporary presence, the young family also had to contend with the ramifications of the Irish Rebellion. Without few exceptions, most of the Catholics in the North supported the Irish Republican Army's quest for independence, and Lizzie and her son were no exceptions. The conflict between religions led to many atrocities with Catholics suffering arson and even machine gun assaults upon their, neighborhoods.

At one point, Lizzie determined that her son had to be placed in the safety of the Hill country while she continued to try to accumulate the necessary means for survival. When that arrangement proved too risky, she had to take refuge among in-laws who resented her incursion, and she soon sought independence despite the perils.

When World War I finally ended with an armistice, she then suffered the challenge of the plague. In 1919 the infamous flu epidemic struck Ulster, with a vengeance. Although she didn't succumb to the flu, her son Richard did. Richard was anointed with Last Rites as a sign of his desperate illness. Lizzie, meanwhile, refused to submit her only son to the ministrations of the Orange doctor believing that the medico would be just as happy to terminate her son's life as save it. She then garnered the aid of a rare Catholic doctor.

In the mining communities of western America, her husband Patrick struggled with his own problems. He had joined the International Workers of the World and was blackballed from future employment. With little recourse, he returned to County Down and still found the job opportunities little improved from his departure eight years previously. Lizzie, however, had become pregnant with daughter Helen, and Patrick resolved to try America again, this time in New York. A half dozen years later, their son Richard, decided to try the land of opportunity himself. Richard, had been mesmerized by the tales of his father and uncles. In 1928, her son, Richard " Dick" emigrated to New York and Lizzie followed him with her young daughter, Ellen in tow. Her reunion with her husband proved short lived for the ravages of working in the mines and drinking to excess led to a premature grave and Patrick died Aug 8, 1931, in Manhattan, leaving Lizzie a widow in a strange land.

As in Ireland, Lizzie tried whatever resources she could to survive in the new Country. She worked as building superintendent since that came with free rent. Now Lizzy was determined that her best chance for survival lay in renting a large apartment and subletting rooms to recent Irish immigrants. When her boarding schemes seemed questionable, she attempted employment in a variety of New York hotels.

Lizzy then enrolled her daughter in the local Catholic School. When queried about her adaptation to the new school, Ellen began to cry and confessed total confusion. Lizzie immediately dragged her reluctant daughter to the school, only to discover that she had inadvertently enrolled her in a German speaking school in Yorkville. With this information, Lizzie at once moved to the Westside and enrolled Ellen in Holy Trinity Catholic elementary school. At school, when asked her name by her teacher, she replied, "Nellie". Not in America, responded the holy Sister. We don't have Nellies in America. Your name will be Helen.

The greatest opportunity arose when America found itself involved in World War II. Women were enticed into the work force and Lizzie found jobs where none existed before. Lizzy was an avid union sympathizer and labor supporter. One of the individuals who could make her blood boil was a scab. An example of Lizzie's behavior, was told by her supervisor in a hotel. He claimed Lizzie would hide in the linen closet until a scab approached in search of clean sheets. Lizzie would then beat her over the head with the heel of her shoe and leave her victim rubbing her wounds.

In New York, Lizzy lived at 869 West 180th Street Manhattan, in the section called Washington Heights. Whenever Lizzy wished to take her grandchildren for a treat, she would have her waist long hair wrapped in a tight bun behind her head. Each night she would unravel her hair as if to signal that she was off duty for the night. She wore only housedresses of the utilitarian kind, not wearing a special dressy gown or having an iota of jewelry. If the weather was cold she donned her hat, fashionable in her eyes, and an overcoat. Lizzy was always called "Nanny". She did not resort to foul language but seemed to have a ready supply of verbal insults to assail her opponents.

Elizabeth Lennon O'Prey died on Aug 17, 1968, after a brief illness at 10960 Nyack, Rockland, New York. Her earthly remains are interred in Calvary Cemetery in Queens, New York.

Donated on 11/24/2016 by Grandson Richard O'Prey
Born in Manhattan, New York, lives in Nanuet, New York
Teacher in New York Public School districts
Widower, 3 children

Jeremiah Sullivan

born 10/9/1854
Bere Island, County Cork Ireland
Parents: Michael Sullivan, Margaret Holland

JEREMIAH SULLIVAN, SON OF MICHAEL Sullivan and Margaret Holland, was born on Bere Island, County Cork, Ireland and christened on the Oct 19,1854.

Jeremiah arrived in Argentina, the exact date of his arrival is not known but it is likely around 1880. He found employment working with the British company which was building the railways in Argentina.

The original construction of the railway began in 1855 and brought vast European immigrants to Argentina. Many came to work on and operate this new railway. The railway was first built with Argentine finances, then it was sold off to foreign private interests, consisting mostly of British Companies. Today it is the 8th largest railway in the world.

We know that in February 1883, Jeremiah was temporarily living in Córdoba, Argentina, because he was present at his sister, Mary Sullivan's wedding as the best man. Mary Sullivan married to Patrick Murphy, both were born on Bere Island, County Cork, Ireland. We don't know, if, apart from Jeremiah and Mary, there were more siblings that immigrated to Argentina. We do know that there were twelve siblings. On the Aug 3,1892, Jeremiah Sullivan married Maria Schmid. Maria was born on Jan 22,1863 in Schärfenberg, (at that time) Austria. According, to the marriage certificate, they married in Tucumán, a northern Argentinian town. I suppose that he was living there at that moment because of his job as railways worker. Jeremiah and Maria had two children: Jerónimo Sullivan, my grandfather, born on the Sept 16,1893, and Francisca Margarita, born on the Sept 18,1895, who probably died short after her birth. I couldn't find her death certificate. Both children were born in Córdoba. In 1895 the family was living in Córdoba, according, to census records.

Jeremiah Sullivan died in Córdoba on the May 12,1897. Patrick Murphy, his bother-in-law, signed as witness his death certificate. At that moment, Jeremiah Sullivan was working as an engine driver for the Railroad.

When Maria Schmid and Jeremiah Sullivan arrived in Córdoba, they settled down in the "English" neighborhood in Córdoba, now Barrio General Paz. Almost all employees and workers from the English railways company were living in this area.

Well, that is the short story of my Irish great grandfather. Unfortunately, we don't have either, pictures, of him or the background why he left Bere Island, Ireland and why he chose Argentina for settling down. My great grandfather died when my, grandfather was a 4-year-old child, and my grandfather died when, my mother was 20 years old, so there are no memories.

Best regards,

DONATED ON 12/4/2016 BY GREAT GRANDDAUGHTER
  MARÍA TERESA LINARES
BORN IN CORDOBA, ARGENTINA, LIVES IN CORK, IRELAND
GERMAN TRANSLATOR, STUDYING ENGLISH AT UNIVERSITY COLLEGE,
  CORK, IRELAND

Michael Connell

born 1844
Kiltycreevagh Townland, Ballinamuck, County Longford, Ireland
Parents: Charles Connell D-4-1855

MICHAEL CONNELL'S, FATHER CHARLES OF Kiltycreevagh Townland, just outside Ballinamuck, County Longford, died according, to Drumlish death records, on April 5,1855.

Michael Connell emigrated from Ireland to Sheffield, England in 1862, and at the age of eighteen, Michael married Bridget Ryan, who was also from County Longford, Ireland, on the April 19,1863 at St. Marie's Roman Catholic Church in Sheffield. The couple had six children in eighteen years, Charles, Thomas, Patrick (died in infancy), Daniel and James, all born in Sheffield. They also had son Martin, who was born in Middleborough, England.

In the late 1800's Michael left Sheffield, England and traveled to America. He arrived in New York City, New York. After he'd established himself, Michael would send for his family to join him. But his family was soon to be informed by letter from a friend in America that Michael had died following asphyxiation in a gas accident. The October 29th 1888 edition of the New York Times, however, reported that James McCabe and Michael O'Connell, farm hands, employed on the grounds of St. John's College, Fordham University, Bronx, New York, were discovered almost dead from asphyxiation by coal gas but were removed to the infirmary and were slowly recovering. Michael never sent for his family to join him in America.

Michael Connell died in New York in 1888. His wife Bridget Ryan Connell died Oct 1893 in Sheffield, Yorkshire, England.

DONATED 11/30/2016 BY GREAT GRANDSON MICHAEL J CONNELL
BORN IN SHEFFIELD, YORKSHIRE, ENGLAND, LIVING IN WHALEY BRIDGE, DERBYSHIRE, ENGLAND
RETIRED INSURANCE COMPANY RISK ASSESSMENT MANAGER.
MARRIED TO EILEEN WITH 3 CHILDREN (ALL MARRIED) – CATHERINE, JAYNE, AND MATTHEW.

Francis Stirling McCracken

born 1860
Abbey Yard, Newry County Down, Northern Ireland
Baptized 1860 in Newry, Country Down
Parents: Robert McCracken, Sarah Elizabeth Gray

ROBERT MCCRACKEN WAS THE NEWRY Steam Packet Commissioner/Agent in Newry, County Down. He provided a scheduled shipping service, carrying freight and passengers. Newry Steam Packet Company was formed in 1871. Newry is a city in Northern Ireland, 34 miles from Belfast and 67 miles from Dublin, it was founded in 1144 alongside a Cistercian monastery.

When his son, Francis was old enough, he left Ireland and went to sea. At the age of 20 years, Francis boarded the ship S.S. Eastcroft and became a member of the ship's crew. He was a very tall man of 5'10 1/4", with brown eyes and brown hair, and his religion was Protestant. He was a Seaman for 12 years and a Carpenters laborer 18 months as an apprentice carpenter. The ship arrived in Sydney, Australia in 1880 and while on leave in 1882, Francis left and never went back to the ship. October 1882 was the Gold Rush Era, and at, this time, there were at least 100 ships in the harbor without crews.

On September 13, 1888, Francis joined the South Wales Water Police, as a Probationary Constable. He was made an Ordinary Constable on September 1, 1898 and became a Constable 1st class on August 1,1893. He was transferred to Metropolitan Foot Police on the August 10,1909 where he worked until his death.

Francis met and married Mary Paterson Duncan on June 4,1891, in 5 East St. Granville New South Wales. Mary was the daughter of Andrew Duncan and Isabella Dobbie. They had three children: Robert Francis b-April 16,1982, Isabella b-May 17,1894, and Mary Elizabeth b-May 17, 1898. His wife, Mary Patterson McCracken died in 1914 and Francis was left to care after the children with the help of young son Robert.

In 1917 Francis met Elizabeth Rose Ethel Madigan. On 11 October 1917, they married in St. Brendan's Church in Annandale. Annandale is a suburb in the Inner West of Sydney, in the state of New South Wales, Australia. Elizabeth Rose Ethel Madigan was the daughter of Mortimer Joseph Madigan and Alicia Thrussel. Elizabeth had five daughters by a previous relationship that she brought to the Marriage. Thelma Irene b-July 8, 1903 born in New Zealand, Elsie Philomina b-Sept 7,1905 born in New Zealand, Vera b-Nov 27, 1907 born in Sydney, Australia, Elizabeth May b-March 16,1911 born in Sydney, Australia, Myra b-May 5,1913 born in Sydney, Australia. Francis and Elizabeth had one son Donald Francis b-July 27,1922 born in Sydney, Australia.

Francis Stirling McCracken died July 13,1925 R.P.A Camperdown, Sydney, New South Wales, Australia and was buried in the Roman Catholic Section Rookwood Section 8 Grave 245, in Sydney, NSW Australia.

DONATED 1/25/2017 BY GRANDSON LAURENCE MCCRACKEN
BORN NSW, SYDNEY, AUSTRALIA
RETIRED CAPTAIN FIREFIGHTER FOR THE FIRE AND RESCUE OF NSW, AUSTRALIA

Patrick Joseph Sheehan

born 4/9/1886
Ballincollig Kielduff, Ballymacelligott, Tralee, County Kerry Ireland
Parents: Timothy Sheehan 1855-1932, Johanna McCarthy 1853-1895

PATRICK JOSEPH SHEEHAN WAS BORN, the fifth of seven children, in a two room thatched cottage in County Kerry, Ireland. His mother Johanna passed away when Patrick was just nine years old. Johanna was the daughter of John McCarthy 1826-1886 and Margaret Ann Sullivan 1824-1881. His father Timothy did the best he could to care for his children, and he did have help from Johanna's parents and Mary Sheehan O'Donnell, who live just next door.

In 1905, at the age of 19 years, with 10 Dollars in his pocket and one suitcase, Patrick boarded the ship S.S. Oceanic, which was the sister ship to the Titanic. He emigrated from Ireland and headed for America, where his brother and an Uncle lived in Indiana. The ship arrived at Ellis Island, New York City, New York. When he departed the ship, Patrick took a train to Fort Wayne, Indiana to his brother John's house. John would help him get employment with the Pennsylvania Railroad Company.

It was here in Fort Wayne, that Patrick met Loretta Agnes Cavanaugh, and on June 4,1914, they married at St. Patrick's Catholic Church in Fort Wayne, Indiana. They had four daughters: Loretta Julia b-1914 Mary Margaret b-1916, Anita Janet Julia b-1921, and Betty Elizabeth b-1926.

Patrick worked for the Railroad for Thirty years, and retired as a Railroad Fireman from the Pennsylvania Railroad Company. Patrick was known as a very friendly sociable man, that would walk thru the town talking to many people. He did not shy away from talking to strangers.

Patrick's wife Loretta Agnes Cavanaugh Sheehan died on Sept 19,1966. Patrick Sheehan died on May 31,1978 and they are buried together in the Catholic Cemetery in Fort Wayne, Indiana.

DONATED 11/28/2016 BY GREAT GRAND NIECE SHELLY SANDS
BORN IN FORT WAYNE, INDIANA, LIVES IN NEWRY, COUNTRY DOWN, NORTHERN IRELAND
MARRIED, 4 CHILDREN

Harris Daniel Zvi Noyek

born 9/3/1873
Uzventis, Lithuania
Parents: Aaron Hillel, Malka Ite Noieck

DURING THE TIME OF ORGANIZED massacres, of particular ethnic groups, especially Jews, following the promulgation of the May Laws of 1881 it had become increasingly dangerous for the Noyek family to remain in Lithuania, even though they had lived there since the 1700s.

In the autumn of 1894, about a year after the birth of their youngest sibling, Daniel Zvi and his older brother Abraham left Uzventis, Lithuania, eventually ending up in Dublin, Ireland. Their journey took more than three years! It had encompassed over 1500 miles, much of it on foot, through Poland, Germany, Holland, and England. Neither one at that time spoke any English - only Yiddish and Russian.

They arrived in Dublin in February 1897, having completed a large part of the travels walking, by train, and in steerage on Lithuanian grain ships. Ireland was then part of the British Commonwealth. When the two brothers arrived in Dublin, there were more than 3,000 Jews in Ireland, primarily of Eastern European extraction.

The Dublin Jewish community at that time was nothing but a handful of (for the most part) impoverished families, who themselves had come as emigrants from Eastern Europe, but in the time, honored tradition of helping other Jews, some members of the community took the brothers in to live with them until they could support themselves. Daniel Zvi took lodgings at the home of Nathan and Sarah Price.

Isaac Noyk, (Daniel Zvi's distant cousin) and his fellow countryman Harry Stein were already becoming established in the impoverished community of Lithuanian Jewish refugees. Isaac's son, Michael (who was born in Luoke, Lithuania) became a famous lawyer, who helped write the constitution of Ireland.

Daniel Zvi's first job in Dublin was in Harry Stein's furniture shop. Although his brother Abraham was a good businessman, Daniel Zvi was more of a scholar and a dreamer. Daniel Zvi became a traveling draper, simply peddling door-to-door on his own. Now anglicized his name to Harris Daniel.

Living in Nathan and Sarah Price home, Daniel got to know their daughter, Eliza (Bessie Gertrude) Price. They became engaged in 1901. Harris Daniel and Bessie G were married March 14, 1902, in Dublin, in a double wedding ceremony, along with his brother, Abraham, and Abraham's bride Molly (Malke) Robinson. Harry Stein was a witness to both weddings. The newlyweds remained in the Greenville Avenue home, where they kept chickens in the back courtyard.

In 1902, Harris Daniel Noyek applied for Irish citizenship, paid 5 pounds and became an Irish citizen on November 22, 1902. Harris's character and respectability where above reproach. He was considered a respectable and law-abiding citizen.

By 1908, Harris Daniel and Eliza had five children, Barney, Tillie, Isadore Isaac (Tommy), and Maurice. They were all born at the family home, which was across the street from Daniel's brother Abraham. When Eliza was pregnant with her fifth child, Rachel, their money situation was very tight. Harris Daniel did not have enough money to support his growing family.

At the turn of the century, the diamond industry, in Kimberley, South Africa had been a "Boom Town". In 1911, Harris Daniel and Solomon decided to go to South Africa to seek their fortunes. Although they had by no means become rich, the Price brothers were at least able to send money back to help the family in Dublin. This was not an unusual decision for Irish Jews in 1911. So many were leaving for South Africa with its promise of wealth, that a portion of the wharf on the North Wall of the River Liffey, became known as the "Wailing Wall of Dublin. This area, was so named by porters working at the docks, because of the streams of women coming there to bid their children and grandchildren "goodbye." These women cried because they assumed that they would never see their children again.

In August of 1914, the First World War broke out. The Kimberley diamond industry, always vulnerable to international crises, was paralyzed by the war. This in turn affected all businesses.

All methods of transportation were cut off, and Harris Daniel and Solomon were neither able to send for their families, nor go back to Dublin themselves. Harris Daniel and the Price family would indeed have prospered, but for the world wide epidemic known as the "Spanish Flu" then invaded Kimberley. Harris Daniel, along with Solomon Stein now faced hard times. During this epidemic, Bessie Gertrude tended to all her Dublin neighbors who were ill, without any thoughts for her own safety.

Harris Daniel finally saved enough money to return to Dublin in 1921. For the first time in 10 years the family was together again. Harris Daniel was a scholarly and religious man, extremely gentle and with absolutely no head for business. His South African experience had destroyed him. His return to Ireland was, in the midst of the Great Depression of the early 1920s and he decided to take over Bessie Gertrude's rent collections. It was a disaster! He would frequently return home with nothing, telling his wife that the people he called on were starving, and needed the money to feed their families. She would ask "and who will feed ours"? Obviously either too proud to seek, or simply unable to get help from Abraham's family, he remained in Dublin working at whatever jobs he could find, including trying to sell clothing from door to door.

An extremely charitable woman Bessie G founded the Dublin Jewish Brides Aid Society (an organization to help women who could not afford to pay for their, own weddings or buy household supplies) in 1939. Bessie G had quite a flair for the dramatic, and had the strongest Dublin accent ever heard. On the day, her sister Emma died in 1947, she stopped dying her hair jet black. As the roots started growing out, she would comment "Look at me - when Emmie died, me hair turned white overnight!"

On June 14,1932 (Hebrew date 10 Sivan,5692, Harris Daniel Noyek died at the family home in Dublin. He was sixty-one. He is buried in the Jewish Cemetery, Dolphin's Barn, Dublin, in Row 1. Bessie G Price Noyek died June 5,1961 in Dublin. Cause of her death was Cancer of the sinus. She is buried in Dublin Jewish Cemetery, Dolphin's Barn, Dublin– Row 8. May they rest in peace.

DONATED 1/15/2017 BY GRANDDAUGHTER DAVIDA HANDLER
BORN DUBLIN IRELAND, LIVES IN HENDERSON, NEVADA
TAUGHT MUSIC, MARRIED, 3 SONS, 8 GRANDCHILDREN

John H Gaffney

born 6/23/1851
Killandy, County Sligo, Ireland
Baptism 7/2/1851
Sacred Heart Chruch, Bunnanadden, Sligo, Ireland
Parents: Thady Gaffney 1824-1894, Bridget Coffey

IN 1872 JOHN GAFFNEY MARRIED Anne McDermott, he was 20 years old and Anne was 19 years old. Anne McDermott was the daughter of Luke McDermott and Anne Doddy of Bunninadden, County Sligo, Ireland. They were married in a Sacred Heart Roman Catholic Church, Bunnanadden, County Sligo.

Sligo is an Irish word meaning "Abounding in shells" because of the abundance of shellfish found in the river. It is a west coastal seaport with the western providence of Connacht, Ireland.

In 1872 John and Anne left Ireland and immigrated to America. They arrived at Castle Garden, New York City, New York. They continued, on to Buffalo New York where there was a very large Irish community. John became a laborer repairing railroad tracks.

Their first son Thomas Joseph aka Peter Thomas was born May 23,1874, then their daughter Mary Anne was b-1876 and daughter Loretta was born in 1877. In 1878, the family went back to County Sligo to live in Bunnanadden with Anne's parents and her brother Rodger McDermott, and his family. They lived in a thatched roof cottage, on a parcel of land owned by Anne's parents, where they farmed the land and also, worked the public house owned by Anne's parents. During their stay, John and Anne were involved in dozens of mishaps, mainly Interfamily fighting, and both landed in gaol (jail) numerous times--along with Anne's father and brother. Some of the charges included attempted murder, numerous assaults, threatening behavior, and attempted assault with a firearm.

Their daughter Elizabeth was born in County Sligo in 1879, and two sons (John and John Joseph) were born but died in infancy. John traveled back to America to find work and eventually came back for the family and they returned to America making Scranton, Pennsylvania their home. John worked numerous jobs with the railroad. Their daughter, Winnifred Agnes was born 1884, and Katie was born 1876 but died in infancy.

Both John and Anne like to drink and are known around town for their drunken, abusive and disorderly conduct. They have regular Citations in the Scranton Republican Newspaper. On one occasion, July 30, 1881, a Police Officer was called to the Gaffney home by Mrs. Gaffney, who said her husband was drunk and threw her out of the house.

Mrs. Gaffney had a badly swollen eye and a cut on her chin. Mr. Gaffney resisted the Police Officer and they were both arrested and taken down to the station house. John Gaffney was called before Judge Gunster to answer charges of beating his wife. Mrs. Gaffney was to be there also, but failed to appear before Judge Gunster. John stated that his wife sustained her injuries when she fell upon a chair after having been overcome by the heat. They jury believed his testimony and acquitted him.

Dec 28,1891, again in the Scranton Republican newspaper, Mr. and Mrs. John Gaffney and Mr. and Mrs. John Boylan, where in the station house under $200 bail to appear in court to answer charges of disorderly conduct. These people are known to the Police as very hard drinkers and when they get intoxicated the bestial part of their nature asserts itself and they fight with each other like dogs. Quite frequently, Mr. and Mrs Gaffney have been behind bars for disorderly conduct. This last escaped was over Christmas celebration held at Mrs. Gaffney's house. At 2am, a neighbor, Mrs. Pilger, went to the Police Station, stating the Boylan's and the Gaffney's were murdering each other. A squad of Police in a Paddy Wagon when to the house, where they found the most deplorable state of affairs. The four persons were taken to jail.

Again, Aug 28,1894, John Gaffney and his wife Anne engaged in one of their, customary fights. During, the course of which the Anne was stabbed in the face by her husband. She required 3 stitches in her cheek to close the wound. They were both arrested and locked up for being intoxicated. On another occasion, Aug, 5 1897, John was charged with stealing $3.75 from the pocket of Patrick Reap. John was held on $200 bail to answer in court.

On Oct 8,1906, the Scranton Repulican Newspaper, reported the death of John Gaffney. John Gaffney, at the age of 55, had taken a job as a Night Watchman for the Laurel Train line and had been employed there for over three years. Mr Gaffney, was said by fellow workers to have a pleasing personality, sunny smile, and a gentlemanly disposition that endeared him to everyone. His boss said he was a valued worker. At the time of his death, John was in pursuit of trespassers on the company's property. He was returning to the office when he was seen to step from one track to another track to get out of the way of an oncoming train. As there were no planks or footwork where he stepped, it was believed that he miscalculated where he should step and fell to his death.

The superintendent was notified and a search crew of six men was sent to retrieve the body. John Gaffney's body was not recovered till 9am the next day. His wake was held at the home of his sister, Winifred Gaffney Murrin, at 916 South Washington St. His funeral was held at the Nativity Church and he was interred in the Cathedral Cemetery. His wife Anne McDermott Gaffney died on Sept 26,1912 of Chronic Endocarditis and was buried with her husband in Scranton, Lachawanna, Pennsylvania.

Donated 12/9/2016 by Great Grandson Timothy Gaffney
Born in Albany, New York, lives in Rottendam, New York
Works as CFO of Private held group of related companies in the Construction Industry.
Married, one son Tim Jr, daughters Kate, and Aryn, one grandaughter Annalise

Peter Kavanagh

born 1850
#28 St. Mary's Terrence, Arklow, County Wickow Ireland
Parents: Peter Kavanagh Sr. Died 1866, Ellen Keough

PETER KAVANAGH SR. WAS THE first Corswain of the Royal National Lifeboat Station in Arklow, County Wicklow. This was founded in 1824. He married Ellen Keough.

CHOLERA IN ARKLOW

To the editor of the Wicklow Newsletter- Death Notice.

Sir, Cholera has carried off Peter Kavanagh Sr., the coxswain of the Life boat, after a few hours, illness leaving a poor helpless wife and eight small children to deplore his loss. Many is the time since the life boat was established here, have undaunted Peter and his brave crew, sped their way to the Arklow Banks to save human life; and often have they rejoicingly brought back their living freight of human beings. It is not long since Peter was presented with the medal of the Institution for his valuable services. Poor fellow, how he loved that medal! He will never save a life again! On Saturday, the 17th, he fell a victim to the pestilence. His widow's case is a poor one; something ought to be done for this brave man's children; and it is to be hoped that those who value worth and bravery, and desire to see them perpetuated, will publicly take up this sad and urgent case. And one wishing to send any help to them could do so by sending it to any of the clergy, Protestant or Catholic. A CORRESPONDENT Nov 21,1866.

Arklow is a town in County Wicklow on the east coast of Ireland. One of the Bloodiest battles of (1798 Rebellion) was fought in Arklow. It is the 3rd largest town in Wicklow, Ireland.

Peter Kavanagh Jr, owned a Railway Tavern in Arklow and he had a small farm on the outskirts of Arklow (Ballymone). Peter met Elizabeth Sheehan, who was born 1864. They were married on Nov 24 1898 and they had seven children. Eugene, Peter, Andrew, May, William, Annie, and Elle. Peter Kavanagh died March 27,1921 and his wife, Elizabeth Sheehan Kavanagh died in 1947 and they were buried together.

DONATED 12/29/2016 BY GREAT GRANDSON PETER EUGENE KAVANAGH
LIVES IN NORTH COTSWOLDS, ENGLAND
AN AUTOMOTIVE ENGINEER WORKING AT THE JAGUAR LANDROVER CAR
  COMPANY
MARRIED, ONE SON

Margaret Anderson

born 1885
Coleraine, County Londonderry, Northern Ireland
Parents: James Anderson

MARGARET ANDERSON WAS THE OLDEST of six children of James and Hessie Anderson. Margaret had four brothers, Robert, Archie, James, Thomas and one sister, Hessie that died in infancy.

he Anderson's lived in Coleraine, which is a very large town 55 miles Northwest of Belfast in County Londerderry, Northern Ireland. It is known for when St. Patrick arrived in the neighborhood, he was received with great honor and hospitality by the local chieftain, Nadslua, who offered him a piece of ground on which to build a church.

Margaret attended St. Patrick Church, in Coleraine, and it is still there today and is the church of Ireland. Margaret worked at Rodgers shirt factory in Coleraine. She was very well educated. Margaret knew William Connor, who was from the neighboring town of Limavady but worked in Coleraine. William Connor was born in 1884 and came from a very poor family and he did not have a lot of education.

In 1910 William Connor left Ireland and immigrated to America to find work. He went to Philadelphia, Pennsylvania, where there was a very large Irish community and he went to live with his relatives, Georgina, and Bob Smyth, that were already living in Philadelphia. William found work with the J. G. Brill Company. This company was founded in 1868 as a horse car manufacturing firm in Philadelphia. He worked and saved up for Margaret's passage and the he sent for her to come to America.

At the age of 26years, when Margaret received the passage money that William sent, she left Ireland and traveled to America to meet William. She never returned to Ireland again. In 1913 they got married and had seven children, all born in Philadelphia, Pennsylvania.

Margaret Anderson Connor died in 1955 and her husband William Connor died 1956. They are both buried in St. James Kingsessing Cemetery on Woodland Ave in Elmwood, Philadelphia, PA.

Donated 1/7/2017 by Granddaughter Louise Connor Wingate
Born 1949 Darby, Pennsylvania,
  Lives in Wildwood Crest, New Jersey
Retired English Teacher, 2 daughters, 3 grandchildren

Mamie Allen

born 1878
Cobh, County Cork Ireland

MAMIE ALLAN WAS BORN IN Cobh, County Cork Ireland. In 1849, Cork was called Queenstown, and it is a seaport town on the south coast of County Cork. Queenstown was the departure point for 2.5 million of the six million Irish people who emigrated to North America between 1848 and 1950.

Mamie Allen met and dated William Anthony Murphy. William Murphy was born in 1877 in the town Bantry, County Cork. Bantry is a town in the parish of Kilmocomoge on the coast of West County Cork. William was going to emigrate from Ireland with his family to Melbourne, Australia and he wanted Mamie to go with him but Mamie refused to move to Australia. William went to Australia with his family and after a few years, he and his family returned to Ireland. On his return, he opened a Shoe Makers Shop. William arrived with a belt of sovereign around his waist and started his shop on Blarney Street in Cork City. Now back in Cork, he married Mamie Allan and they lived in Cobh, County Cork, then they moved up to Cork City where they started their family. They had four daughters, Frances, Madgie, May and Nellie and one son Michael, who was born in 1909.

One of William's specialties was making Fairy shoes, he was quite the expertise Cobbler and he made these shoes for a big Exhibition in Cork. Today those shoes are in a museum. The last pair of shoes that William made were passed down in the family. William died in 1911, when his son Michael was just 2 years old. The climate in Ireland killed him.

Now Mamie was left to raise five children by herself. She did struggle, as her Money was invested badly. Mamie loved the Opera and she had beautiful penmanship. Everyone that could not write, went to her to have forms filled out.

She lived to 90 years old and died in 1968. William Anthony Murphy and Mamie Allan Murphy were buried together in Curraghkeppane Cemetery in Blaney Road, Cork City, County Cork Ireland.

DONATED 1/1/2016 BY, GREAT GRANDDAUGHTER
 FRANCES IRENE MURPHY
BORN IN CORK CITY,IRELAND,LIVES IN ESSEX ENGLAND
MARRIED, 2 SON, 1 DAUGHER, 4 GRANDCHILDREN

Hugh Hodges

born 1892
Clannaghey, South West Tyrella, County Down, Northern Ireland
Parents: Henry Hodges, Christina Cummins

HUGH HODGES MET AND MARRIED Sarah Toner, whom he knew from Clannaghey. They had two children; Christina Elizabeth Sarah Hodges; born April 20,1914 and Elizabeth Sarah born two years later in 1916. Hugh was employed as a Gamekeeper in Tyrella before joining the Royal Irish Guards, 'C' Coy; 8th/9th Battalion as a Rifleman.

While fighting in Cambria, Ypres, Belgium, Hugh was shot in the back while Rescuing his injured comrade. Subsequently treated at Bath Hospital in England. His wife, Sarah went to the hospital right away to be by his side. She also brought his small daughter Christina to be by his side, leaving his daughter Elizabeth home with her parents. Sadly, Hugh Hodges lost his life to his terrible injuries on Nov 23,1919. He received the Military Medal for his valor. However, his father was adamant his son, Hugh, was not to have a soldier burial as he detested the Great War and having lost one of his son's, to it and therefore had his body buried in the family grave at Rathmullan Church of Ireland to a humble burial.

Hugh left behind a wife, Sarah, and two small children; both who ironically married English Soldiers when visiting Northern Ireland; and all of them including Sarah Toner Hodges set up home in England. Sarah Toner Hodges never married again, and lived with one of her daughter's until she was in her 80's.

Clare Ann Conway

Donated 1/12/2017 by Great Granddaughter Corine Leighton
Born in Stockton on the tees, Cleveland, England
Married, Housewife, Children Stephanie Leighton, James Leighton

Kate Sheridan

born April 17/1889
Cavan Town, County Cavan Ireland
Parents: Patrick Sheridan, Anne Clerkin

KATE SHERIDAN WAS FROM CAVAN Town, County Cavan near the border of Northern Ireland. Cavan was founded in 1300 by King Giolla Íosa Ruadh O'Reilly.

Kate met Michael McCallion who was born on December 24, 1882 in Tieroneil, Ballindrait, Donegal and was the son James McCallion, a farmer and his wife Mary Hageny. Michael, Mick as he was call, was a railway engineer and during his rail travels he lived in Cavan where the rail hub was located. They married in 1911.

They both wanted a better life then they had and decided to go to America where Mick had a brother, James living in New York City. In April 1911, Mick set sail for New York City, New York where, he was sponsored, by his brother James, who had come over the year before. In 1912, Kate with her baby Anna set sail to join Michael in New York. Kate and Mick welcomed baby Mary, who was born in March of 1913 and baby Agnes arrived in May 1914.

Mick found work as a New York City trolley car driver and in December 1913 he was on a run, on Fort George Hill in New York when the car crashed and he was badly injured, caused by a fire on the trolley car he was assigned to. Several days later he died of his injuries and left Kate at home with two baby daughters and another on the way.

James, Mick brother sent word to Ireland about the accident and word came back that Mick's Mother, Mary, would be happy to bring baby Mary home to Ireland to raise her. Kate said she preferred to raise her own daughters and so she did. Kate maintained a very close relationship with James and his family, but Kate did not keep contact with her husband's older relatives back in Ireland.

Kate was left with three children and life became a bit challenging. She did manage to raise her three daughters with hard work and perseverance. Kate worked as a laundress, for a very wealthy woman. She was faithful in keeping in touch with her family in Cavan Ireland and always sent a little something home to her Mother. In 1944, her Mother died and the family was lost to those in New York. Life intervened and the families in New York and Ireland forgot each other.

Kate always said she had a very good life even though she spoke Mick's name to someone every day. Her daughters and granddaughter were with Kate when she passed. And while she was only a child, the granddaughter recalled Kates last words to her daughters. She smiled and said Mick is here for me and I must go.

Kate Sheridan McCallion died in New York City on November 22, 1957 at the age of 67 from diabetes. All the McCallion's from Ballindrait, Donegal Ireland, who arrived in America are buried in Calvary Cemetery in Queens, NY. That would be, Michael McCallion, his wife Kate, as well as his brother James (Jimmy) and his wife Annie Mcbride McCallion

In about 1965, Kate's great grandson was a NYC Policeman and moonlighted by driving a cab on Long Island, in order, to support his growing family. One day whilst driving he happened to pick up a young woman with a distinct Irish brogue. Upon questioning the young passenger in his cab, she indicated that she came from Cavan and of course the conversation turned to his Mother and Granny coming over to America in 1912 from Cavan. At that point the ride took a very dangerous turn when the young woman pulled a photo out of her bag and passed it over the seat to him, saying she was out here several years ago, looking for her Auntie Katie. Who would believe that the photo was his own Mother and his Granny Kate? He was lucky he didn't drive off the road. The Families were once again reunited.

Donated 1/14/2017 by Granddaughter Fran Miller
Born in Yonkers, New York, raised on Long Island, New York
Married, settled upstate where my husbands, family has lived since 1710.
2 grown sons and four grandkids. Two boy and two girls.
Recently retired and am enjoying spending more time with my grandkids.

Thomas Joseph Donovan Sr

born 10/11/1884
Ballydevlin, Goleen, County Cork Ireland
Parents: Andrew Donovan 1838-1919,
Eliza Wilcox 1843-1983

IN THE SMALL RURAL VILLAGE of Ballydevlin, Goleen, Andrew and Eliza Donovan had lived thru the Great Hunger in County Cork Ireland, along with their parents, neighbors and friends. They had seen all the hunger, death, and misery and survived.

Goleen is on the south-west end of the Mizen Peninsula in the tip of Ireland. Farming was the main occupation of the town people.

The Donovan family home in Ballydevlin --- the big house was on the ocean with a marvelous view --- the original smaller house is now a hay barn ---- all on a cliff, actually ----- and there was a small break in the cliff, (called a boreen) so that's how they got the boats out to go fishing. They were primarily fishermen, as well as well, known poets. They also had the farm, cattle, fields with wild horses for racing. One uncle owned a "Keep" - a small castle –

Andrew and his wife Eliza were blessed with a very large, close knit and loving family, of 14 children. Mary b-1866, Michael b-1867, Patrick b-1870, William, Kate b-1871, Andrew b-1873, (Twins) Daniel b-1873, Elizabeth b-1876, John b-1879, Jeremiah b-1881, (Twins) Hannah b-1881, Annie b-1882, (Twins) Ellen (Nellie) B-1882, and Thomas b-1884

At the age of 24 years their son Thomas Donovan had decided to leave Ireland and he headed for America. He boarded the ship S.S. Arabic out of Queensland and on Oct 4,1912 arrived in Boston, Massachusetts.

Thomas moved from Ireland to the United States at a time when immigrants were expected to quickly assimilate into American Society. From Boston, he continued, to Lawrence, where he lived in a factory for a while.

He met Helen Regan in Lawrence, Mass., who was also from Goleen, County Cork. Helen was born in 1886 on the small Island (Long Island) off the coast of Cork. They could both see the same lighthouse, when they were growing up. She came to America with her parents at the age of 13yrs. on the ship S.S. New England on May 17, 1899 and arrived in Boston, Massachusetts. Her family settled in New Bedford, Mass. In Lawrence Thomas and Helen married in 1919. He was 34 years and she was 25 years old. They then moved to New Bedford, Massachusetts. Thomas never learned to drive a car, living in the City, he took the bus everywhere.

New Bedford was a factory town with lots of work for immigrates. He went to work in a Cotton Mill then, Thomas found work in the Coaters Incorp. Leather Factory on 139 Potter St. New Bedford, Mass. Thomas was in charge, of the temperature of the room. Leather needed to be kept cooled.

In June 1919, Thomas's father Andrew Donovan passed away at the age of 81 years in Goleen, County Cork Ireland. His Mother Eliza Wilcox Donovan also passed away in 1919 at the age of 76.

Thomas and Helen married and lived at 222 Smith Street, New Bedford. They owned the house and they did all the painting and papering of the inside. They had a very large vegetable garden in their back yard. They had a summer cottage in Fairhaven, Massachusetts.

They raised seven happy, wonderful children, all born in New Bedford, Mass., Ellen b-1920, Margaret b-1922, Josephine b-1924,

(Twins) Thomas b-1924, Andrew b-1928, Theresa b-1929, Patricia b-1935. Education was very important. All, of the children graduated High School and 2 Graduated College. All the children went to 12 years of Catholic School.

Thomas Donovan put salt on everything at every meal. It's amazing that he lived to the age, he did. He ate mountains of it every day, and lived a vital and busy life until the age of 93 years. Thomas eat potatoes every day and vegetables out of his own garden. He was still saving for his old age at the age of 92 years. He spoke Gaelic and all his children did also. They would swear in Gaelic also.

Thomas taught his daughter Patricia to knit with her fingers. Back in Cork Ireland it was how they mended their fishing nets (with their fingers). Thomas was a great story teller and recited poems. He didn't talk much about growing up in Cork. If he did, they were not very pretty stories. Families were forced out of the homes with their, belongs by the side of the road. Houses were set on fire by the Black and Tans. He told, of his brother that had a Pub in Cork City.

In 1931 he was crushed and hurt by an elevator. His wife Helen, went out the same day, working on an estate on the ocean in Fairhaven, Massachusetts.

Thomas Joseph Donovan died in Feb 1978 at the age of 93 years and his wife Helen F Regan Donovan died Nov 7, 1983 at the age of 97 years. They were buried together in New Bedford, Mass.

DONATED 1/11/2017, BY DAUGHTER PATRICIA DONOVAN 82 YRS OLD.
3/29/1935.
BORN IN NEW BEDFORD, MASSACHUSETTS, LIVES IN GUILFORD,
CONNECTICUT
MARRIED, RETIRED

Bridget (Bessie) O'Hara

born February 2, 1885
Toocananogh, Bohola, County Mayo Ireland
Parents: Martin O'Hara born 1850,
Mary Dunleavy born 1846

BESSIE O'HARA LIVED IN THE very small village of Bohola, Westport, County Mayo. Bessie immigrated to America on the ship S.S. Umbria and arrived at Ellis Island, New York on May 13, 1906. She continued, on to Chicago, Illinois where she would live with her sister Julia. Here in Chicago, Bessie met Peter Frank Bullinger. Peter Bullinger was from Germany. They married and had seven children.

In Chicago, Peter owned his own Auto Repair Shop. " Bullingers Auto Repair ", Peter was a Master Auto Mechanic. Peter F Bullinger died in 1932. Bessie O'Hara Bullinger died December 1968, in Lake Zurich, Illinois.

DONATED BY GRANDDAUGHTER JULIE REID
BORN IN EVAN ILLINOIS, LIVES IN BABB MONTANA
MARRIED, HAS 2 SONS AND 7 GRANDCHILDREN
SHE IS RETIRED U.S. CUSTOMS PORT DIRECTOR AT THE US/ CANADIAN BORDER

James Patrick Dinnen

born 1894
Aughavas, County Leitrim Ireland
Parents: James Patrick Dineen b- 1837,
Mary Ann Curran b-1840

JAMES PATRICK DINNEN WAS A tenant farmer under British Rule in the southern part of County Leitrim in a small town of Aughavas. He and his wife Mary had eight children, Charles, Thomas, James, Mary, Margaret, Patrick, and William and Ellen. They rented the farm they lived on. James Patrick was born in the town of Curraglass, and his wife came from Carrigallen, County Leitrim, Ireland.

Another resident of County Leitrim, James Murtha, had immigrated to the America in the early 1900s, leaving his sweetheart, Kathleen Cantwell, behind. He arrived in Oregon and made his way to Condon in Central Oregon, where after a few years he was able, to buy the sheep ranch he managed. As an early entrepreneur, in addition to his ranch, he acquired several other properties.

In 1910, James returned to County Leitrim to ask his sweetheart, Kathleen, to become his wife and move back with him to his ranch in Oregon. While still in Ireland, James Murtha approached Charlie Dinnen to join him in America as his straw boss to manage the laborers and sheep back at his ranch in Condon. Charlie left by ship from County Cork with James Murtha and his bride.

Astoria, Oregon, is on the Pacific Ocean at the mouth of the Columbia River with a rich history of immigration, beaver fur trade, and salmon canning. Condon is up river and inland a couple of hundred miles from Astoria. In September 1910, the Condon Globe Times newspaper documented the arrival of James Murtha and his new bride, accompanied by Charles Dineen and others, all from Ireland.

In 1911, Charles's brother, Tom, immigrated to America to the east coast, landing in Boston, Massachusetts, before he travelled across country to join his brother in Oregon on the Condon Ranch.

March 15, 1912 brother James Dinnen left Ireland from Queenstown in County Cork and boarded the ship S.S. Lusitania for America. He landed in Boston, Massachusetts to find a better life and freedom. He would eventually join his brothers, in Astoria Oregon. James left his three sisters, Mary, and Margaret, and Ellen back in Aughavas, and they would join the brothers later when they got settled. James was a poet, singer, and an early entrepreneur. He wrote a poem, "A tribute to a loved schoolmate" that was published in the local newspaper.

On April 1920, James and his brothers Tom and Charlie purchased a ranch from John Murtha. The ranch that they purchased was 6,800 acres, sheep Ranch. It included the house, barns, equipment and 5,000 head of sheep at a cost of $90,000. This was a lot of money for three Irish brothers with no apparent savings.

In May 1920, the two Dinnen sisters, Mary and Margaret arrived from Ireland. The Dinnens held a big party with dancing and singing when the sisters arrived. Dances consisted of Jigs, Reels, and Horn pipes. Some neighbors and friends, in attenance were Mr. and Mrs. Tom McIntrye, Mr. and Mrs. Perkins, Miss Bea Carrico, Miss Lizzy Creegan and Phil Newman to name just a few. It was also written up in the local newspaper that the sisters had arrived.

Tragedy struck in July 1920. James was found drowned behind the house in Lone Rock Creek. James Dinnen died at the age of only 26 years old.

World War I, which started in 1914. To meet the needs of our troops, the U.S. government contracted with farmers and ranchers all over the States for grains and meats – chickens, beef, sheep, and other foods. There was a rapid growth of ranches in Christmas Valley near La Pine and south of Bend, Oregon. At the peak of the war, there were several hundred ranchers employing over 3,000 folks to provide meats to our troops. At the war ended in November 1918, there were still troops in many places, and the United States government continued providing foodstuff for them in the States and Europe.

WW 1 ended in late 1918 but there was no armistice agreement signed, so our, government kept purchasing food from farmers all over the country. In that third weekend on September 1920 an agreement was signed. The U.S. government cancelled all purchasing agreements with farmers, over- night. Tens of thousands of farmers went, bust. Farms and animals were abandoned with no hope of the future.

The Dinnens abandoned the Ranch the third weekend in September 1920. They moved on to Spokane and Walla Walla, Washington and then to Dalles, Oregon. The ranch remained abandoned for 20 years until the Dinnens sold the ranch to John Monahan for $10 in 1938.

DONATED 1/23/2017 BY NEPHEW PAUL LYONS
BORN IN PORTLAND, OREGON, LIVES IN LAKE OSEWEGO, OREGON
MARRIED, 2 ADOPTED GROWN CHILDREN, 1 SON, 1 DAUGHTER
RETIRED CONSULTANT AND RESEARCH ANALYST

John Moran

born 4/3/1857
Milltownpass, County Westmeath Ireland

JOHN MORAN WAS BORN IN Milltownpass in Westmeath, he was a farmer and laborer. Milltownpass is a village in the south of County WestMeath. It was one of the first villages in Ireland to have an Electricity supply. A Mill on the Milltown River provided power for the village long before Rural Electricity arrived.

John met and married Catherine Whelehan, she was born in 1864 and was also from Milltownpass, just down the road from John. They had thirteen children. John and Catherine loved traditional Irish music and their door always unlocked. Many of the neighbors and friends would come into their home for singing and dancing. John would play a comb-like, harmonica.

About 1890, John departed Ireland and went to Liverpool, England. In Liverpool he boarded the ship S.S. Cephalonia for America, and arrived in Boston, Massachusetts. When he got settled he sent for his wife Catherine.

Catherine came with only three of their children, Mary, Martin, and John, to Boston, leaving the others back in Ireland. They only stayed in Boston for a few years. Their daughter Mary, became ill back in Ireland. They left Boston on the ship S.S. Cephalania and arrived on Aug 14, 1894 in Liverpool, England, and continued, on arriving home in Ireland. At the age of 12 years, Mary died in their home village of

Milltownpass, of Pulmonary Fibrosis. After the death of their, daughter, John, and Catherine never left Ireland again.

John Moran died May 15,1934. John and his Catherine Whelehan Moran are buried in the old cemetery in the Rochfortbridge parish, Milltownpass, in County Westmeath, Ireland.

DONATED 1/22/2017 BY GREAT GR GRANDSON
    NATHAN JAMES STANIFORTH
BORN IN SHEFFIELD, ENGLAND. LIVES IN TEXAS, USA,
DATA ANALYST, MARRIED

Thomas McCracken

born 1770
Drumahorgan, Magilligan, County Londonderry,
Northern Ireland
Parents: John McCracken 1750, Isabell Caldwell

THOMAS MCCRACKEN WAS BORN IN Drumahorgan, Magilligan, in Northern Ireland. Drumahorgan is in the Civil Parish of Magilligan. Magilligan is a peninsula in the Northwest county of Londonderry, Northern Ireland. In the mid1700s Magilligan was separated up in to different family sections. The McCracken's were farmers and in 1775 the Doughs section of Magilligan, was given to John McCracken and his wife Isabella Caldwell.

Thomas McCracken met and married Elizabeth Docherty. They married at Dochertys home at the Doughs in Magilligan. Both the McCracken and Docherty families belonged to the Church of Ireland but the McCrackens left to join the Presbyterians Church in 1820.

Thomas established the Drumahorgan farm, and the family still owns it today (2017). Thomas and Elizabeth had four children: George b-1811, Caldwell b-1812, Mary Anne b-1818 and Arthur b- abt. 1820. Thomas's Mother Isabell helped take care of the children.

Thomas McCracken died in 1864 and is buried with his wife Elizabeth Docherty McCracken at the Magilligan Presbyterian Church.

DONATED 1/28/2017 BY GREAT, GREAT GRANDSON
 STEPHEN MCCRACKEN
BORN IN LIMAVADY, COUNTY ANTRIM, NORTHERN IRELAND
MARRIED, 2 CHILDREN, WORKS FOR UNITED DAIRY FARMERS

Joseph McCracken

born 12/25/1819
Limavady, County Derry, Northern Ireland
Baptised Drumachose Presbyterian Church, 27 Church St. Limavady
Parents: Joseph Solomon McCracken, Mary Quiq

JOSEPH MCCRACKEN WAS BORN IN Limavady which is a market town in County Londonderry, Northern Ireland. He had learned the trade of Tannery and worked with animal hides.

At the age of 21 years Joseph and his parents left Ireland and they sailed to America where they had relatives in Indiana County, Pennsylvania, and cousin's in Philadelphia, Pennsylvania.

In Philadelphia Joseph met Mary Ann Hunter. They were married on Dec 26,1848 by Rev. John R. Nichols. Witnesses were Mrs. Nichols and Thomas McIntyre. Mary Ann Hunter was also born on July 12, 1830 in Ireland.

When Mary Ann Hunter was a baby, her parent's house, was struck by lightning and caught fire. The house burned and her mother died in the fire. Mary Ann was saved when someone carried her in her cradle from the burning house. Her father later remarried to a lady who had a son by a previous marriage. Mary Ann's step-mother mistreated her for years. In 1844 Mary Ann decided at the age of 14 years. she wanted leave and go to the America. Her step-brother worked and provided her passage. Mary Ann arrived in Philadelphia, Pennsylvania all alone. While standing on the dock crying and bewildered, a gentleman named Chadwick noticed her plight and offered her a job helping his wife in their home and with their store. She was said to live with this couple until she met and married Joseph McCracken.

Shortly after their marriage, Joseph and Mary Ann traveled to Indiana County to the area then known as Kelleysburg, Pennsylvania. Here Joseph started a tannery. He had this profession for several years until his attentions turned to agricultural endeavors. He purchased timbered land in the northern part of Indiana County. He cut down the logs and built his first house, then spent the balance of his life tilling the soil.

Joseph and Mary Ann had nine children: David John, b-Jan 27,1850, William Alexander (Alex) b-Mar 21,1852, Mary Elizabeth (Lizzie) b-Feb 28,1854, Anna Jane (Annie) b-Nov 2,1855, Sarah Margaret b-Dec 15,1857, Joseph James b-Sept 23,1859, Hugh Pollock b-May 4,1862, Samuel Thomas b-June 18,1865, Emma Nancy b-Aug 22,1868.

Joseph and Mary Ann were members of the Methodist Episcopal Church of Rochester Mills. Joseph was an elder of the church and Mary Ann was a member of the W.C.T.U. In his later years, Joseph had snow-white hair combed in the fashion of George Washington. He drove a fine buggy pulled by a snow-white horse.

Mary Ann Hunter McCracken died Feb.12, 1897 at their home in Grant Township Indiana County, Pennsylvania. On March 28,1905 Joseph sold the family farm to his youngest son, Samuel Thomas. Joseph had lived with his daughter for three years prior to his death. Joseph McCracken died Dec 30,1907. Joseph, his wife Mary Ann and their son Hughey were buried together in the Pine Grove Cemetery, Rochester Mills, Indiana County, Pennsylvania.

DONATED 1/27/2017 BY GREAT GR GRANDDAUGHTER
REENE MCCRACKEN MOCK
LIVES IN HOMER CITY, PENNSYLVANIA
MARRIED, 2 SONS, 2 STEP DAUGHTERS, 11 GRANDCHILDREN, 5 GREAT GRANDCHILDREN.

Charlotte Glass

born 1863
Tamlaght Road, Rasharkin, County Antrim, Northern Ireland
Parents: Matthew Glass 1821, Charlotte McMilan

THE ORIGINAL FAMILY GLASS CAME to Ireland from Scotland in early 1700's on a small farm along the river Bann, located between Kilrea and Portglenone in the Barony of Kilconway. The Bann River is the longest River in Northern Ireland.

Three Glass brothers farmed in neighboring farms. Times were hard and the brothers worked long hours on the farms. They had a lint dam, processing the fiber for Irish linen which would have been weaved on their farm and neighboring farms. They would take the linen by horse and cart to the market town of Ballymena for the train journey to Belfast to be loaded on the cargo ships bound for America. The brothers made the red clay Bann bricks on the riverside fields and had their own brick kiln, the bricks would then be loaded onto barges along the river Bann and sold, the rejected bricks were used for building and repairing their homes, some of which were built from field stones and as time went by the old houses underwent many renovations as the family's wealth improved so did their furniture and belongings.

The autumn of 1842 claimed many lives in the local area. They lost children in the famine and watched neighboring families die out. The local farms saw the crops fail and illness spread claiming the life of young Robert Glass, a son who should have been the heir to the family farm.

Samuel Glass did inherit the farm and willed it to his brother Matthew when he died.

Mathew married Charlotte McMillan a local lass and they shared the family home with his mother, Mary. They had bought his brother William's farm at the beach trees when he moved to Rasharkin as the local Blacksmith. Rasharkin is a small village in County Antrim in Northern Ireland. Matthew Glass and his wife Charlotte were both born in this local town.

Matthew and Charlotte brought their children up on the farm. They were taught to read and write by both parents and they helped, out on the farm. On Sundays they would visit Church and attend Sunday school at Portglenone Presbyterian Church.

The young Charlotte Glass named after her mother enjoyed working in the milk House where she churned the milk from the family cows and made butter. The butter milk was, used by her mother to make soda bread farls over the griddle which hung from the crane over the open turf fire. Soda bread farls are commonly eaten with sausages, bacon, fried eggs, pudding, and fried tomatoes.

Even the turf would have been hand cut in the summer months by the family and stored to fuel the fire for cooking and heat in the thatched stone cottage. The Glass cottage, at this, time consisted of two rooms on ground floor and an open loft on first floor accessed by a step ladder.

Charlotte would often help her mother and grandmother Mary crochet lace collars with fine bone or wood hooks. These remain at Charlotte's homestead to this very day along with the lace she crocheted. They had their own spinning wheel and a quilting frame on which many beautiful quilts.

About 1885, their daughter, Charlotte Glass and her sisters Eliza and Melinda Immigrated to America. In the late 1890 sisters Margaret Ellen and Agnes followed them. Charlotte and her sisters made their way to

California and found work as housekeepers. In 1900 a brother Samuel also immigrated but all communication with him was lost.

Charlotte wrote regular letters back home to her family. She sent many letters to her brother Hugh and his wife Rosetta and their children. Hugh stayed behind in Ireland with two other sisters. At Thanksgiving, each year Charlotte would post a parcel home to her brother and sisters to receive for Christmas.

After a few years, Charlotte traveled to and settled in Little Rock, Arkansas. She never married. Charlotte did travel home to Ireland often by boat until she injured herself in a fall and passed away. Letters from Ireland tell of how Matthew and Charlotte Glass lost all their, daughters, and one son to America. Charlotte was the only child to return to Ireland. Her other Sisters, never did return to Ireland but they all did well in America.

To start, Agnes stayed in Orange Grove, Los Angeles, California, marring a Mr. Harris. Her sister Melinda married Oscar Jones and Eliza married Samuel Faires and had a son and two grandchildren. They all lived close to Charlotte and would spend Thanksgiving and Christmas together.

Margaret Ellen married into the Cockram family and had a daughter called Bertha (Peg) Margaret Ellen stayed in California. Peg married into Schneider family and resided at Ocean Boulevard, San Diego, California.

Agnes settled in Sask, Nebraska. All these Glass family girls had been great at crochet lace collars and cuffs and sent them home to Ireland often. Their, mother Charlotte and father Mathew Glass never left Ireland, owning farms. When the parents passed away back home, the children all sent money home to have a memorial grave stone erected in the finished marble.

Charlotte Glass died in her home at 5119 B Street, Little Rock, Arkansas in the late 1950's no record of death found.

Information on Charlotte Glass was obtained from letters found in her home belonging to Noeleen Glass given to Clare Conway for her book.

DONATED 1/30/2017 BY NOELEEN GLASS
BORN LEMAVADY, COUNTY ANTRIM, NORTHERN IRELAND
MARRIED, 2 GIRLS, 2 BOYS, 1 GRANDDAUGHTER, 1 GRANDSON
OWNS AN INTERIORS DESIGN BUSINESS

John Murphy

1821
Newry, County Down, Northern Ireland
Parents: George Frederick Murphy, Margaret Murphy

IN SEPTEMBER 1843 JOHN MURPHY and his wife Mary and daughter Margaret, boarded the ship S.S. Elizabeth from the port of Cork, County Cork, Ireland which was bound for Sydney, Australia with 1500 passengers from Newry and County Down. John a Presbyterian and a carpenter by trade and as there was no work in Ireland, John took his family to Australia to find work and make a new life.

On January 20,1844, they arrived and disembarked at Sydney. They were sponsored by Mr. William Walker, who was a shipping agent. Mr. Walker had also provided the family with lodgings at Kent Street. Arriving at Sydney, the Murphy's were now a family of four. Mary had given birth to a son at sea.

John has established himself as a prosperous oil and color Merchant. He traded at 23 Parramatta Street, which was 100 yards from the Railroad Station. If you wanted to paint your cart, coach, or house, your needs would be met with comparison prices. John's business prospered and expanded during the 1860's. The business became John Murphy and son, and they expanded to 21-23 Parramata St. (Today it is George Street).

John was now appointed an agent for the British Plate Glass Company. He now does large print advertisements which boost his business. He has the Largest showroom, the largest and best selection of stock, and the most practical Staff in the colony.

John Murphy is closely associated with the International Exhibition where his Honor Sir James Martin, seriously doubted there was a sufficient quantity of glass and iron procurable in Australia. John Murphy wrote the following letter to the editor of the Sydney Morning Herald.

John Murphy and son now 35years of experience in the business, is recorded as supplying many of the Glass Cabinets for the International Exhibition. The firm was entrusted with the work of fitting up a large number of showcases, in the "Garden Palace" with British Sheet and plate glass, some of it was very large, in size. Many of the finest looking cases in the British and Colonial Courts have thus been fitted up. As we think that His Honor in this view scarcely does justice to the importing enterprise of the colony in respect to glass, we beg your permission to state that owing to the rapid yet steady expansion of trade in the colony, improvement in means of communication with Europe and the keen competition of our merchants, the magnitude and variety of stocks in warehouses and afloat required now, is such as to enable us to undertake very important works without special importations. As proof of this, we could guarantee to supply glass for such a building as intended for the Exhibition, punctually and without interference with our ordinary trade."

With confidence and determination John had laid the foundation for a successful business venture since the first day he arrived in Sydney, Australia. He worked hard and made prudent investments and became a well, respected Business man. He earned the respect of his employees who gave him a banquet in his honor in 1877.

John Murphy died on Oct 19,1880 and is interred at Rockwood Cemetery, Old Catholic section, area 5, mortuary 1, Vault 1, Sydney, Australia. He left behind his wife, four daughters and two sons.

DONATED 2/5/2017 BY GR GRANDDAUGHTER KERRIE CARLE
BORN IN SYDNEY, AUSTRALIA, RETIRED SCHOOL LIBRARIAN ASSISTANT
MARRIED, 2 DAUGHTERS, 1 SON, 1 GRANDSON

Ellen Maher

born 12/22/1829
Killenaule, County Tipperary, Ireland
Parents: James Maher, Margaret Harris
Married 5/15/1828

ELLEN MAHER MUST HAVE BEEN in a workhouse to be considered for the famine orphan scheme as according, to the shipping records she is listed as a farm servant, religion Roman Catholic with her parents still alive and living in Killenaule so, her parents must have been extremely poor for her to be classed as a Famine Orphan.

On December 6, 1849 Ellen left Ireland in the ship the "John Knox" with 278 other Irish Famine Orphans and arrived in Sydney, Australia on April 29, 1850 after 144 days at sea sailing via the Cape of Good Hope.

In Sydney, Ellen met John Cecil Heimrich (Henry) Bachfeld at the Bachfield Family Hotel where she worked. Henry Bachfeld had arrived on the ship S.S. Bloom on July 7, 1852 from London, England from his home country of Germany by way of Antwerp Belgium. He was a Butler and later he changed the spelling of his name to Bachfield. John Bachfeld was from a wealthy family in Cassel in Hesse, Germany and his brother owned the Musson Perfume Factory. Henry was the owner of the "Bachfield Family Hotel on Castlereagh Street in Sydney. He later went into the business of importing Liquor and cigars from Europe with a Belgium Joseph Dhanis, but this business was unsuccessful and Henry went insolvent in 1857.

John and Ellen married on July 15, 1854 at St. James Church in Sydney. On Aug 21, 1855 their first daughter Margaret Elizabeth Josephine Bachfield was born at the Bachfield Family Hotel.

Ellen had sent for her sister Mary and brother Thomas to come to Australia and paid 5 pounds each for their passage. In 1856 Ellen's 16 years, old sister Bridget, and 22 years, old Thomas arrived on the ship S. S. Commodore Perry. However, Mary arranged her own passage and gave her ticket to her sister Mary. Ellen and Henry are living in the Family Hotel and when Mary, Bridget, and Thomas, arrive they live at the Hotel also.

On July 16, 1859 Bridget married Joseph Edmond Francois Dhanis at St. Mary's Catholic Cathedral in Sydney. In 1860 they have a daughter Cornelia and in 1861 the move back to London, England, and have a son Francis Ernest Joseph Dhanis. They then went to Greenock, Scotland, where Joseph set up a shipping Company before returning to live in Antwerp, Belgium. In May 22, 1892 Bridget Maher Dhanis died.

Ellen's sister Mary married George Gall in 1858 and they had four children. Her sister Margaret married George Koch in Tenterfield Catholic Church May 1867 and they had seven children. Brother Thomas married Mary Hickey who was from Tipperary, Ireland in 1859. They had twelve children. Thomas died of Typhoid in April 1889.

Henry and Ellen had eight children: Margaret b-1855, Gertrude b-1856, James b-1859, Elinor b-1861, Henry b-1864, Augusta b-1865, Alice b-1868, And Mary Minna b-1872.

In 1859, after being bankrupt for the 2nd time, Henry, Ellen and their three children left Sydney and moved to Tenterfield in the New England area of New South Wales, Australia. The family went to live at Wilson's Downfall where Henry tried his hand at Tin Mining. Henry became Mining Warden's clerk and bailiff of the small debts court at the

Tenterfield Court House. This position he held for 20 years and retired on Jan 9, 1903.

John Cecil (Henry) Heinrich Bachfield died on July 22, 1905 at the age of 78 years. After her husband death, Ellen suffered from dementia and lived with her youngest daughter, Mary Minna Bachfield Worboys. Ellen Maher Bachfield died on Jan 24, 1907. They were buried together in the Old Tenterfield Cemetery, New South Wales, Australia.

DONATED 2/4/2017 BY GREAT GRANDAUGHTER
  JOY LORRAINE WORBOYS
BORN NORTH SYDNEY, NSW, AUSTRALIA MARRIED
WORKS FOR ESTATE AGENTS AND SOLICITORS (LAWYERS)

Mary Agnes Joyce

born 2/3/1888
Manulla, County Mayo Ireland
Parents: Michael Joyce 7/22/1838,
Mary Reddington 3/1/1863

THE JOYCE'S WERE FARMERS IN County Mayo and Mary Agnes was one of five children. Their farm was located, between Balla and Castlebar. Manulla is a famous little Town that St. Patrick visited and built a church in. Before St. Patrick arrive this whole area was Pagan.

In 1908 Mary Agnes went to America with her brother Thomas, to live with an Uncle Dennis Joyce. After her stay, Mary Agnes returned to Ireland but her brother Thomas stayed with their Uncle Dennis. On Oct 1920 Mary Agnes immigrated to America, this time to Chicago, Illinois area to live with her Aunt Mary. This city also had a very large Irish population. At, this time, her brother Thomas and her Uncle Dennis relocated to Chicago, so they would all be together.

In 1921, in Chicago, Mary Agnes met Martin Fadden, who was also from Mayo, Ireland. Mary Agnes is now 33 years old and they marry on April 6, 1921. Mary Agnes Joyce Fadden died in Chicago, Illinois on July 1,1962.

DONATED 3/25/2016 BY GRANDSON AUSTIN FADDEN
BORN IN CHICAGO, ILLINOIS, LIVES IN KNOXVILLE TENNESSEE
MARRIED, 2 BOYS, 2 GIRLS, RETIRED

Thomas Moore

born 1858
County Cavan, Ireland

THOMAS MOORE WAS BORN IN County Cavan, Ireland. Some areas of County Cavan were hard hit by the Great Famine potato blight between 1845-49. The winter of 1847 had high levels of deaths nationally caused by diseases such as typhus and cholera. Several instances of eviction also occurred during the nineteenth century, with one such story where the local landlord in Mountnugent parish decided to evict over 200 people.

Cavan borders six counties: Leitrim to the west, Fermanagh and Monaghan to the north, Meath to the south-east, Longford to the south-west and Westmeath to the south. Cavan is the 19th largest of the 32 counties. Cavan is known as 'The Lakeland County' and contains 365 lakes. It has a very hilly landscape and contains the Bellamont Forest.

In Ireland, at age 18, Thomas Moore was in the RIC, Royal Irish Constabulary. It was the armed police force of the United Kingdom in Ireland from the early nineteenth century until 1922. Thomas Moore married Catherine Cameron. In 1881 Thomas and his wife left Ireland and immigrated to America and arrived in New York City, New York. They continued, on up to Minnesota and settled in the southern part of the state, in Jackson County.

In Minneapolis, Minnesota, Thomas found work as a bricklayer in the local brickyard. Catherine gave birth to their daughter Catherine, born in Jackson County Minnesota in 1881.

In later years, his daughter Catherine married Victor Lloyd. Catherine Moore Lloyd died in 1949 and her husband Victor Lloyd died 1941 and they are buried at St. Mary's cemetery in South Minneapolis, Minnesota. Thomas Moore died in 1934 and is buried at Heron Lake Minnesota with his wife Catherine Cameron Moore.

Donated 2/19/2017 by Gr Great Grandson Shawn Vernon Lloyd born in Minneapolis, living in St Paul, Minnesota, unmarried with no kids.

Bridget McQueeny

born 1831
Drumshanbo, County Leitrim Ireland
Parents: John McQueeny, Mary Kelly

THE MCQUEENY FAMILY WERE VERY poor and the ended up with their children going to and residing in the Workhouse in Drumshanbo. The Workhouse was built in 1840 and was declared fit for admission of paupers on July 1, 1842. With the potato famine and a young family to raise John and Mary decided to send their daughters overseas and give them new lives.

Bridget McQueeny was one of eight children. Bridget, who was 18 years old and her sister Mary, who was 17 years old, were sent to Australia as part of the Earl Grey program. They went to England and boarded the ship S.S. Lady Peel out of Plymouth on March 14,1849. The girls arrived in Sydney, Australia on July 6,1849 as Famine Orphans. Neither Bridget or Mary could read or write. From Sydney, they made their way to Brisbane, where Bridget found work as a housemaid.

In Brisbane Bridget met William Bowden. William was the son of John and Ellen Bowden, born in 1818 in Cheshire England. He arrived in Brisbane on the steamer S.S. Eagle and he was a convict brought over from England. His occupation was a Miner in England. William and Bridget married in Brisbane at St. Stephen's Church on Dec 26 1849. They were married by, the first resident Priest of Brisbane. They traveled northwest on a Bullock Dray (a Truck or a cart pulled by Bullock or a young Bull) and settled on the Auburn River where William build a slab hut with a shingle roof.

When their first son John was born, William was away, Bridget gave birth without any assistance and by the time William returned Mary had cleaned herself up and was in bed with her new baby boy.

William now worked as a carpenter and they moved to the Colinton area which is 86 miles north of Brisbane. Over the next nine years they had seven more children and then the family moved to the Laidley area, where William worked a small farm. He grew oats, barley, maize, potatoes, and pumpkins.

On July 3,1871 William was kicked in the head by a horse and died from his injuries. He was buried with no headstone for the lack of money. Seven months later Bridget gave birth to a daughter.

After the death of her husband, Bridget and her family moved to Hope Creek which was just outside Roma in the Western District of Queensland, Australia. This is where she raised her children and when they married, Bridget helped raised her grandchildren.

Bridget McQueeny Bowden died Nov 12,1908 and is buried in the Bowden Burial plot at the Roma Cemetery. Bridget raised twelve children and had eighty-six grandchildren.

DONATED 2/27/2017 BY GR GREAT GRANDDAUGHTER JENNIFER ROOKS
BORN IN DALBY, QUEENSLAND, AUSTRALIA
MARRIED, 3 SONS, 3 GRANDCHILDREN, RETIRED FROM EDUCATION

Margaret (Maggie) Cahill

born 1894
Cregg, Balla, Co Mayo Ireland
Parents: Patrick Cahill, Mary Foy
Married Strade Chapel, Alauskey, Co Mayo

MARGARET (MAGGIE) CAHILL WAS THE youngest child of twelve children. Maggie's Mother died from complications of childbirth a week after she was born. Her older sister Maria was the one to raise and take care of Maggie. In 1901, when Maggie was 7 years old, Maria took her to America aboard the ship S.S. Teutonic to visit and stayed with a sister that lived in, Brooklyn, New York, and they stayed for five years.

In 1907 their Father passed away so they went back home to Bella, Ireland. Maggie got a job as a servant, helping in the home of the John Egan family. The Egans lived, in Swinford Town, County Mayo Ireland.

In 1912 Maggie left Ireland to go back to New York. She was, suppose, to be on the Ship Titanic, but didn't get to the port on time, so she took the next ship, the S.S. Adriatic. She arrived in New York on April 27, 1912. This time she stayed with her brother Patrick. Most of Margaret's brothers and sisters now lived in America.

Maggie did go back to Ireland and met Joseph Paolini. They married on May10, 1920, and had two children, Joseph, and Gloria Paolini.

Maggie Cahill Paolini, died in Ireland in 1960 at the age of 66 years.

DONATED 3/15/2016 BY GRANDDAUGHTER VIRGINIA (GINNY) MARTIN
BORN IN BROOKLYN, NEW YORK. LIVES IN CALIFORNIA
MARRIED, 2 DAUGHTERS, RETIRED

Dorinda Florence (Dot) Moriarty

born 1885
County Galway, Ireland
Parents: James Bowen Moriarty 1848-1930,
Margaret Emily Topham 1857-1934

DORINDA MORIARTY WAS BORN IN the harbor city of Galway on Ireland's west coast. Galway is one of the largest cities in Ireland. During the famine, Galway had food riots because of the food shortages in 1842.

Dorinda had gone to Dublin Ireland and in 1912, met Arthur Ortestes Grey. Arthur was born in 1884 in Hong Kong China. They married in 1912 and had one son.

Dorinda Moriarty Grey died March 19, 1959 in Belfast Ireland at the Royal Victoria Hospital. This hospital is a landmark building and claims the first air-conditioned public building in the World in 1906. Her husband Arthur Grey died in 1980 in Belfast Ireland.

DONATED 3/14/2016 BY MARY JANE KIRBY
BORN MELBOURNE, VICTORIA AUSTRALIA, LIVES IN COCKATOO,
    MELBOURNE
WORKED AS A RECEPTIONIST FOR A DOCTOR'S OFFICE
MARRIED, 2 SONS, RETIRED

Elizabeth (Eliza) McQueeny

born 1836
Drumshanbo, County Leitrim Ireland
Parents: John McQueeny, Mary Kelly

THE MCQUEENYS WERE VERY POOR and in 1840 a new Workhouse was built in the small town of Drumshanbo. The Workhouse opened in 1842 and the McQueenys with their children ended up going to and resided in the Workhouse. This was a very hard time during the potato famine and the McQuennys had no land or money. John and Mary McQueeny wanted their children to have a better life and sent their older children away.

Eliza sisters Margaret and Ann went to America. Sisters Bridget and Mary went to Bisbane, Queensland, Australia. Bridget met and married a William Bowden and Mary met and married James Cash.

In 1854 Eliza's father John McQueeny died and was buried at the Drumshanbo Famine Cemetery which is just on the outskirts of the city. He was buried in a paupers grave with no headstone. The cemetery entrance is through the old gate of the Drumshanbo Famine Graveyard. Eliza's father was buried with some 500 other victims of the Great Famine. A rosary hangs from a tree in the center of the cemetery. In 1856 Eliza with her Mother Mary, sisters Catherine and Alice, and brother John, left Ireland to travel to Australia to live with her sisters Bridget and Mary and their families. Her brother-in-law paid for their passage to go to Australia.

In Australia Eliza met Thomas Laffin. Thomas was born in County Kilkenny and he migrated to the Colony of Queensland, Australia on the ship S.S. James Ferney in 1855. Eliza and Thomas married and settled on the Darling Downs. Darling Downs is a farming region on the western slopes of the Great Dividing Range in southern Queensland, Australia. The area is dominated by rolling hills.

Here Thomas ran a Carry Company. He and Eliza had a family of ten children, five that lived to adult. Thomas started to lose his eyesight and was going blind. He had gone to Brisbane for an operation. Then he went to Sydney and Melbourne for eye treatment. Thomas also had traveled to London and Dublin for eye treatments. Now with no money or property, Thomas was still blind and unable to work. Thomas was admitted to the Dunwich Benevolent Asylum in 1878. He had to leave his wife Eliza and child in Dalby.

Over the years, Thomas had several unexplained periods of leave and on Feb 1888 he was discharged to leave. He was readmitted to Dunwich, where he stayed until his death on July 14, 1894.

After Thomas's death, Eliza met James Arthur French. They married on Dec 4, 1909. Elizabeth (Eliza) McQueeny Laffin French died on Jan 28, 1929.

DONATED 2/27/2017 BY JENNIFER ROOKS
BORN IN DALBY, QUEENSLAND, AUSTRALIA
MARRIED, 3 SONS, 3 GRANDCHILDREN, RETIRED FROM EDUCATION

Thomas Adams

born 1844
Cootehill, County Cavan Ireland
Parents: James Adams 1815-1889, Jane McCullough.

COOTEHILL IS A MARKET TOWN and townland in County Cavan, Ireland. It is an Irish word meaning "the sleeve". In 1837 it became the site of one of the first eight branches of Ulster Bank which remains to this day. The Cootehill workhouse was built in 1841-2, to accommodate up to 800 inmates and a fever hospital was added in 1846 during the Great Famine.

In 1865, Thomas met and married Isabella Kelly. Isabella was the daughter of Robert and Jane Kelly of Cootehill. At the time of his marriage, Thomas was a farmer at Drumleague, Parish Drumgoon, Cootehill. They were both 21 years old.

On June 10, 1865, Thomas and Isabella left Ireland on board the ship S.S. Tudor, a vessel of 1785 tons, arriving at Lyttelton, Christchurch, New Zealand on September 24, 1865. It was an Assisted Emigration. They paid £28, £17 in cash and £11 was paid by the Provincial Government.

Lyttelton is a port town on the north shore of Lyttelton Harbour, at the north-western end of Banks Peninsula and close to Christchurch, on the eastern coast of the South Island of New Zealand. In August, 1849 it was officially proclaimed a port. Thomas and his wife settled in Christchurch which is the largest city in the South Island of New Zealand, and started their family. Thomas and Isabella had 12 children: Jane 1866-1949, James 1868-1872, Isabella 1870-1957, Robert 1872-1872, William 1873-1957, Eliza 1876-1958, John 1876-1955, Evalene

1878-1968, Thomas 1880-1917, Margretta 1882-1937, Mabel 1884-1982, and Francis 1885-1916.

Thomas Adams died of inflammation of the lungs in Christchurch on December 8, 1885 at the age of 41 years. He had been a farmer and had lived in New Zealand for 20 years. He had a staunch adherence to the Presbyterian faith. Thomas was buried in the Addington Cemetery, Christchurch. When he died, the shock was very severe to the wife and family.

Isabella was left with ten children aged from 16 years to 6 weeks. There were six girls and four boys with the youngest a babe in arms, the oldest girl Jane, was 16 years, and the oldest boy William, was 12 years. With no widow's pensions given in those days and no other help such as is given today, what a prospect lay before Isabella and her ten children and very little in the way of worldly, goods.

She did not rebel against her fate and her god. She had a deep trust and faith in God. To her the first line of the 23rd Psalm "The Lord is my Shepherd I shall not want" was not mere words, it was real - a promise she trusted in all her days.

One of Thomas's daughters, Margretta, aged 2 years, wore a pair of black gloves which she kept all her life as a reverent and loving memorial to her father.

After Thomas's death, Isabella lived in Belfast, near Christchurch, with her Children. Belfast is named after Belfast in Northern Ireland. They were Subsistance farming, growing and selling what they could. Isabella and the older children took care of the large vegetable garden, fruit trees, cows, chickens, and hens that they lived on.

Isabella Kelly Adams died in 1920 at the age of 76 and is buried in the Addington Cemetery, Christchurch, New Zealand, with her husband.

DONATED 3/8/2017 BY GREAT GRANDDAUGHTER BARB SILINGER
BORN IN DUNEDIN, NEW ZEALAND IN 1947, CURRENTLY LIVES IN DALYELLUP
MARRIED, TWO SONS AND ONE DAUGHTER, RETIRED FRENCH TEACHER

Alexander Dunn

born 4/20/1833
Aghabog Parish, County Monaghan

ALEXANDER DUNN WAS BORN IN Aghabog Parish, in the union of Cootehill, in the County of Monaghan, and province of Ulster. The town people were nearly all involved in the manufacture of linen.

In March 1860 Alexander Dunn decided to move his family to America for a better life. When Alexander Dunn first arrived in America he settled with his wife Margaret and two young children in Clermont County, Ohio. Alexander was the third member of this family to come to Ohio. He was one of seven siblings, a sister Elizabeth and a brother John, came to Ohio before him and he choose to join them. Later another brother, William, also moved to Ohio in 1869 from Ireland. The Dunn's were Presbyterians. They were descended from Scots who moved to Ireland from Scotland in the 17th century and known as Ulster Scots.

This was the start of America's Civil War between the States. Seven Southern Slave states individually declared their secession from the U.S. to form the Confederate States of America. War broke out in April 1861 when Confederates attacked the U.S. fortress of Fort Sumter

On July 2,1863 Alexander enlisted in the Ohio National Guard. He served as a Private in Company D of the 153rd Regiment Ohio Volunteer Infantry in the Civil War. He was mustered into service in the newly created 153rd Ohio Regiment on May 2,1864 at Camp Dennison, Ohio.

On July 14, 1863, General John Hunt Morgan led approximately 2,000 Confederate cavalrymen into Clermont County as part of an attempt to draw Union forces away from the southern conflicts. Morgan's Raiders, as they became known, crossed the Little Miami River at Dungan's Crossing, and attacked bridges, railway lines and trains across the state before leaving.

Alexander Dunn and his Regiment spent most of May and June performing guard duty at Harper's Ferry, West Virginia and along the Baltimore and Ohio Railroad.

The 153rd Ohio Volunteer Infantry Regiment was a 100-day regiment called up in the spring of 1864 to support President Abraham Lincoln's plan to achieve victory over the Confederate armies and bring an end to the War for Southern Independence.

Colonel Israel Stough commanded the 153rd Regiment of 909 men. The Regiment was strung out along approximately 35 miles of the Baltimore and Ohio Railroad, in Hampshire County, West Virginia where the rail line followed the winding Potomac River as through heavily forested and rugged mountain terrain in the lower Shenandoah Valley.

During his service with the 153rd Ohio Regiment Alexander Dunn was promoted to Corporal on June 10,1864. He was admitted to hospital in Cumberland, Maryland for intermittent fever on August 2,1864. Approximately one week later, on August 10, he returned to duty. His military record also indicated he was 5' 8" in height, with a light complexion, hazel eyes, and auburn hair.

Confederate cavalry brigades struck the 153rd on two occasions in July. In the First a force was sent to destroy the railway bridge over the South Bridge of the Potomac at its confluence with the North Branch. Led by Brigadier General John Imboden's, Northwestern Virginia Brigade, the considerably larger Confederate forces encountered a union scouting party and captured 34 men and killed one officer of the 153rd enroute to the bridge.

On July 6, the 153rd was attacked by the Confederate brigade at the bridge at Big (Great) Cacapon and successfully defended it. They were also attacked the same day at the railroad bridge at Sir John's Run but beat back the Confederates with assistance of ironclad railway cars under the command of the 2nd Maryland Regiment.

At the end of July, Colonel Israel Stough and the 153rd were moved to Old Town, Maryland on the Potomac River to block a Confederate withdrawl across the river into West Virginia. The 153rd lay in the path of McCausland's force of approximately 3000, cavalry and a heavy artillery battery. The battle started on August 2 and initially Colonel Stough was successful in throwing the Confederates back, however, with superior numbers they were able, to flank the Ohio troops. Colonel Stough, retreated, back across the river with the 153rd to the blockhouse at Green Springs, West Virginia. The 153rd received support there from the 2nd Maryland Regiments with an ironclad car but Confederate artillery knocked it to pieces.

The confederates completely, surrounded the blockhouse and demanded Colonel Stough surrender. They agreed upon surrender the Union Soldiers would be released and permitted to transport the wounded by hand car to Cumberland. This was the last documented engagement of the Civil War for the 153rd Regiment in which Alexander Dunn served. When the Regiment was mustered out on Sept 9, there remained just 753 men.

After his service in the American Civil War, Alexander Dunn returned to Clermont County, Ohio. However, he did not remain there. His wife Margaret Mills, who he had married in 1857 before leaving County Monaghan, Ireland, for America, died in November 1870 near Cincinnati, leaving three children: Mary Elizabeth, who became proprietor of a hotel in Elkhorn, Colorado, Alexander, who went gold mining in the Cripple Creek gold region, he married Josephine Crozier, a widow, of Claremont, Ohio, and had six children, Mary, Frank, Thomas, Arthur, Charles, and Clarence. And John, who graduated in 1897 from the law department of Colorado State University in Denver and became a United States Senator from Alaska.

Alexander relocated to Cass County, Iowa in 1872. In 1893 to a farm he was the First to occupy and improve in Cedar Township. For many years, he was a Justice of the Peace in Iowa. He was re-elected to the office for three terms, or six years in Cass County, two terms in Calhoun County, and served three terms in Cedar Township. He received a pension for his service in the Civil War.

Alexander Dunn died on Feb 10,1909 in Pochontas, County Iowa at the age of 71 yrs.

DONATED 3/15/2017 BY GREAT NEPHEW BRIAN EDWARD MCCONNELL BORN IN OTTAWA, ONTARIO, LIVES IN DIGBY NOVA SCOTIA, LAWYER

- Just wondering -

FOR YEARS, I HAD ASKED "How did we survive when so many thousands died"? No one could answer me but I kept asking. On the Internet, I asked on a Irish Website page. I was told, "You Yankee, you don't know your own Irish History". (Shameful) But it wasn't taught when I went to school in America. I kept asking, someone tell me what you know. I want to be informed, I want to try to understand. One person came on and said, "Not everyone that wore a British uniform was British". I didn't like hearing that. I guess, if you were hungry and couldn't get work and had no money to feed your family that you would put on the British uniform and evict your neighbors. (Disgraceful)!

They threw the sick and elderly out into the cold, babies and whole families out to die with no place to live. Many people that built their own stone houses from scratch. Back then people didn't or couldn't (ordinary folks that is) own their own land, but rented it from Landlords who were mostly English. Some landlords more heartless than others.

Families from Murrisk, County Mayo, where they were not allowed to fish. From what I know, if you were caught 'poaching' it was a crime. Poaching could mean jail or being sent to Australia. What a way to have to live!

The other thing was that any boats they had, they sold, for food ironically. It was one way of making a living that you could have survived on. Yet the British didn't care.

I started to ask cousins. One cousin told the story of her Grandfather. My oldest Great Aunt, married a man O'Connor for Galway, an interloper. He liked to go to the races. The neighbors didn't like him at all. He met and became friends with the Marquis of Sligo, Mr. Brown, a landlord in Mayo, Ireland, that loved the races also.

My family had rented land from him in Laghloon, Westport, County, Mayo Ireland. The Conway's and McGreal's and the Gibbon's, were all cousin and given land by this Marquis of Sligo. So now I'm bothered. You mean to tell me, that because a Conway was friendly with the Marquis, we weren't evicted? I'm sure we paid our rent but this was a terrible thought (in my head). The Marquis didn't evict the families of his friends? This was a shocking thought that popped into, my head. I really didn't like either one of these scenarios. And I still wonder how we survived when thousands and thousands died. I believe the cousins all took each other in when a spouse died and shared cows and milk and eggs and other foods.

We survived and moved on to America, everyone still, keeping, in touch with all the cousins up to today 2017. I may never know how my family survived such hard cruel times in Ireland but I do know, if we don't keep these memories going, and keep retelling the stories, one day the tragedy, desperation, and inhumanity will all be forgotten. 2/4/2017 Clare Ann Conway

Thousands are sailing by Andy Irvine

You brave Irish heroes wherever you be
I pray stand a moment and listen to me
Your sons and fair daughters are now going away
And thousands are sailing to Americay

So good luck to those people and safe may they land
They are leaving their country for a far distant strand
They are leaving old Ireland no longer can stay
And thousands are sailing to Americay

The night before leaving they are bidding goodbye
And it′s early next morning their heart gives a sigh
They do kiss their mothers and then they will say
Farewell dear old father we must now go away

Their friends and relations and neighbors also
When the trunks they are packed up all ready to go
Oh the tears from their eyes yhey fall down like the rain
And the horses are prancing going off for the train

When they do reach the station you will hear their last cry
With handkerchiefs waving and bidding goodbye
Their hearts will be breaking on leaving the shore
Farewell dear old Ireland will we ne′er see you more

Oh I pity the mother that rears up the child
And likewise the father who labours and toils
To try to support them he will work night and day
And when they are reared up they will go away

Andy Irvine, Permission 3/30/2017

CPSIA information can be obtained
at www.ICGtesting.com
Printed in the USA
BVOW06s1325220917
495656BV00014B/73/P